# The Reminiscences of Detective-Inspector Christie

J. B. Castieau

Alpha Editions

This edition published in 2019

ISBN : 9789353804992

Design and Setting By
**Alpha Editions**
email - alphaedis@gmail.com

This book is a reproduction of an important historical work. Alpha Editions uses the best technology to reproduce historical work in the same manner it was first published to preserve its original nature. Any marks or number seen are left intentionally to preserve its true form.

The "Told-by-the-Pioneers" Series

THE

REMINISCENCES

OF

DETECTIVE-INSPECTOR

CHRISTIE

RELATED BY

J. B. CASTIEAU.

GEORGE ROBERTSON & COMPANY
PROPTY. LTD.
MELBOURNE, SYDNEY, ADELAIDE, BRISBANE
and LONDON

DEDICATED

TO

SIR HARRY N. P. WOLLASTON,
K.C.M.G., I.S.O., LL.D., J.P.

*Elliott & Fry, London, Photo*
Sir Harry N. P. Wollaston, K.C.M.G., LL.D., I.S.O., J.P.
Comptroller of the Customs Department of Victoria and Comptroller General of the Trade and Customs of the Commonwealth.

*Facing page 4*]

# CONTENTS

|  | Page |
|---|---|
| Preface | 7 |
| Biographical Introduction | 9 |

**Part I.—As a Detective.**

| Chap. | I.—Initiation | 19 |
| ,, | II.—Halliburton's Robbery | 24 |
| ,, | III.—Robberies | 35 |
| ,, | IV.—Brookes and Wilson, Coiners | 42 |
| ,, | V.—O'Grady's Robbery | 47 |
| ,, | VI.—Catching a Forger | 50 |
| ,, | VII.—An Opera Singer's Jewels | 54 |
| ,, | VIII.—The "Snowbird" Case | 62 |

**Part II.—As Royal "Shadow."**

| Chap. | IX.—The Visit of Prince Alfred, also of the Duke and Duchess of York | 73 |

**Part III.—As Champion Athlete.**

| Chap. | X.—A Pugilistic Interlude | 89 |
| ,, | XI.—Heavy-Weight Championship | 99 |
| ,, | XII.—Champion Sculler of Victoria | 103 |

**Part IV.—As Customs Detective.**

| Chap. | XIII.—Illicit Distillation | 113 |
| ,, | XIV.—The Last of the "Moonlighters" | 130 |
| ,, | XV.—The "Widow's" Perambulator | 136 |
| ,, | XVI.—The Coffin Trick | 143 |
|  | A Bogus Illicit Still | 144 |
| ,, | XVII.—Women Smugglers | 148 |
| ,, | XVIII.—The Gentle Art of "Crimping" | 160 |
| ,, | XIX.—Opium Smuggling | 170 |
| ,, | XX.—Bridge and Its Consequences | 183 |
| ,, | XXI.—Story of a Diamond Necklace | 206 |
| ,, | XXII.—Miscellaneous Customs Frauds | 212 |
| ,, | XXIII.—"A Cloud of Witnesses" | 218 |
| ,, | XXIV.—The "Language" of Birds | 228 |
| ,, | XXV.—Conclusion | 231 |
| Index |  | 235 |

# LIST OF ILLUSTRATIONS.

| | | |
|---|---|---|
| J. M. Christie | | Frontispiece |
| Sir Harry N. P. Wollaston | Facing Page | 4 |
| Seal of the Christie Family | ,, | 9 |
| Christie as a Swagman | ,, | 28 |
| Christie as a "Christy Minstrel" | ,, | 29 |
| Christie Watching a Suspected Dwelling | ,, | 48 |
| H.R.H. the Duke of Edinburgh | ,, | 72 |
| Christie as a Sailor on H.M.S. *Galatea* | ,, | 73 |
| Christie and Ned Devine | ,, | 83 |
| Christie and the Commissioner of Police, N.Z. | ,, | 84 |
| T.R.H. the Duke and Duchess of York | ,, | 86 |
| Christie v. Hicken Prize Fight, 1876 | ,, | 96 |
| Christie as Champion Sculler | ,, | 102 |
| Detectives and Police in the Western District | ,, | 112 |
| Christie Sells the "War Cry" | ,, | 113 |
| Christie as a Travelling Tinker | ,, | 116 |
| ,,   ,,   ,, | ,, | 117 |
| Reading Warrant to Tom Delaney | ,, | 117 |
| A Newspaper Portrait: Lord Hopetoun as Christie | ,, | 128 |
| Smugglers and their Dodges | ,, | 170 |
| Detective-Inspector J. M. Christie | ,, | 212 |
| An "Old Hand's" Tribute | ,, | 234 |

# PREFACE.

THE life of every mature human being contains the material for a book, and sometimes many books, provided records have been preserved. The volume may be one of romance, history, adventure, or the stirring events of an active life. There the book is, if only we can get the facts, and thereon base the story. Fortunately Mr. John Mitchell Christie was as methodical in this respect as he was in everything he undertook. He carefully kept notes and newspaper cuttings of all the incidents, official and athletic, in which he has played a part. As, in a period covering nearly forty-five years, he was successively a leading Victorian Detective, a Royal "Shadow," Champion Oarsman and Boxer of Victoria, and Detective-Inspector of Customs during a specially interesting period, it will at once be recognised that his career must have been crowded with interesting incidents. The following pages have been compiled from a mass of records and personal narratives. The task was not easy, because the wealth of material made selection a problem. For Mr. Christie's career contains many books, which might be spread over a scope bewildering in its variety. It was decided finally to select and relate events in their order of date, so that the narrative, even though some of the items are separated by years, are yet in chronological sequence. What is given here is representative of the man and his eventful career, and may perhaps prove an appetiser for a fuller feast to follow.

For reasons which will appeal to every reader, the correct names of some persons who appear in these pages have been withheld. The few instances need not be particularised, as they are readily recognisable.

## BIOGRAPHICAL INTRODUCTION.

JOHN MITCHELL CHRISTIE was born at Clackmannan, in Scotland, in the year 1845, and came from a family distinguished in active public service from generation to generation, as the crest and motto "Pro Rege" indicate. His grandfather was a Major of Brigade in Canada, where he married a beautiful and accomplished Irish girl, daughter of an Irish officer in the French Army. Captain James Christie, his father, served in India, and on retiring settled at Clackmannan. John Mitchell's brother, also a Captain James Christie, belonged to the 42nd Highlanders, the famous Black Watch. He was present at the siege and capture of Lucknow, and other important engagements of the Indian Mutiny. Subsequently he was Governor of Edinburgh Gaol, facetiously known as "Christie's Hotel." That there is much in the tradition that "blood will tell" these pages should further testify.

Young J. M. Christie was intended for the Army, and to that end, at the age of seventeen, was placed at Taylor's College, Woolwich, after a preliminary education at Madras College, St. Andrews, Scotland. At Woolwich he was conspicuous as being the only Scottish pupil.

This caused some of the other scholars to attempt to make him a butt. In resenting this he encountered the bully of the school, and a fight was arranged. It was no mere schoolboy "scrap," but a regular set-to with ring, seconds, and a referee, who was a Sergeant-Major in the Royal Marine Artillery. Christie fought pluckily, but was beaten. On going home for the holidays he found that his father had been fully informed of the affair. But instead of censure, he got encouragement, for Captain Christie was a "sport" in the truest British sense of the word, having himself had some experience of boxing in the Army. "We'll fix you up so that you will be able to lick that fellow when you go back," he declared, and thereupon took his son away to London, where he put him with Nat Langham, a celebrated pugilist, who, in his day, had defeated the renowned Tom Sayers. Young Christie came through his course of lessons with a straight, strong left, some sound advice as to P.R. tactics, and a special prescription for the treatment of "rushers," of whom the bully was one. Then he returned to school, where the old feud broke out afresh. Another battle royal ensued, in which the previous result was reversed. Christie's bit of science enabled him to thrash his opponent, and the victor was carried shoulder-high around the school ground by his delighted comrades.

This incident is related at length, because it is one which considerably influenced one of the most interesting phases of Christie's career. It is only such incidents which it is proposed to pick out in this brief biographical sketch.

When the Woolwich term ended an unexpected change

## BIOGRAPHICAL INTRODUCTION.

was made in the family's intentions in regard to Christie. His mother's brother, Mr. Hugh Reoch, was heard of from Australia, where in Gippsland, Victoria, he had made successful ventures in squatting and mining. This uncle practically proposed to adopt his nephew and make him his heir. After grave consideration this tempting proposal was accepted and all thought of the Army abandoned. So, saying farewell to his family and friends forever, Christie took passage in the *Commodore Perry* to seek his fortune 16,000 miles away. He arrived at Melbourne after a ninety-three days' voyage, and immediately proceeded *en route* to Sale by the steamer *Keera,* then commanded by Captain Patrick, the veteran and popular bay excursion boat commander.

At Sale he was met by Mr. A. C. Pearson, and later on by Mr. William Pearson. The latter subsequently became one of the foremost public men in Australia. He was elected to the Legislative Council, which entitled him to the prefix "the Honourable." As owner of such celebrated Australian horses as Commotion, Plausible, and others, he became prominent in the racing world, while as a director in the famous Walhalla Long Tunnel Gold Mining Co. he acquired a further great influence, being particularly popular with the men, for whom he obtained a rise of 10/- a week in wages. He befriended Christie throughout their acquaintance, and it was a piece of rare good fortune that the young immigrant should so soon after arrival have found so solid a friend.

Horses had been brought for the party to ride to the Pearson homestead, Kilmany Park, and then Christie commenced his course of painful new-chum experiences. He had never ridden on horseback before. But he braced himself up for the ordeal, and, with the aid of a by-stander, got astride his lofty mount, a famous thoroughbred steeplechaser named "Wandering Willie," upon which Christie recalls that he felt like a "Jumping Jack."

This was only the opening of a series of bush experiences, which ended in turning him out an expert rider, oarsman, and all-round bushman, a proficiency destined to prove invaluable to him in after years, when his duty took him through the roughest country under the roughest of camping conditions.

The next move was to Stringer's Creek, now best known as Walhalla, where he was to meet his uncle, Mr. Reoch, who immediately initiated his nephew into the various phases of mining life from prospecting to reefing. Various prospecting ventures proved unprofitable, and the nephew was sent to Bolden's Station at Strathfieldsaye to learn station life. The life did not suit him, although the lessons of his experiences were not lost. It was during this period that a few daring adventures on the Gippsland Lakes in precarious boats, made him familiar with the handling of water craft, and no doubt contributed towards his subsequent success as a sculler. He and his companions also had some exciting encounters with wild pigs, and incidentally had to flee from the wrath of an irate farmer whose tame domestic pigs they had slaughtered in mistake. There followed many other mining ventures which were failures, during which at Mount Pleasant he met Mr. Walter Butler, a well-known goldfields warden in his day. Mr. Butler was a character. An expert huntsman himself, he never opened a gate where he could take a fence.

## BIOGRAPHICAL INTRODUCTION.

He had all his paddocks gateless, so that when the frequent importunate seekers of horse accommodation came along he could always say, "Certainly, if you can get into the paddock!" Very few ever could. Among other things he was a deadly shot, and would hit a bucket being carried by his man servant, also a character, and a Crimean veteran known as "Mickey Free." The latter would sometimes be tossed a crown-piece, which he would hold up in his hand to be shot out of it by his master. Mickey's reward was the crown. Once being asked if he was not frightened, Mickey characteristically replied, "Shure, why should I be? The boss is so good a shot that he could not hit you if he thried!"

There now happened another incident, which led to Christie's development as a fighter. On the goldfields was Tom Curran, ex champion pugilist of Victoria. Attached to the hotel he kept was a room devoted to boxing, among the patrons being then Chief Justice Stawell, Mordaunt Smallpage, William Pearson, and other prominent public men. These induced Curran to arrange a meeting between Christie and a noted prize-fighter known as "The Bruiser," to whom Curran jokingly described the new chum as a counter-jumper. "Oh I'll soon settle Mr. Counterjumper," replied "The Bruiser," but, as it happened, it was he who was settled, being knocked-out in nine rounds.

Shortly after this, news came of the drowning under tragic circumstances of his uncle Mr. Reoch. It was found that a will had been left making his nephew heir to his estate. But it had not been witnessed, and was therefore invalid. So Christie was suddenly thrown upon his own resources. There could be no more indefinite dabblings in mining and station life. He must at once seriously consider a settled career. Finally he decided that, notwithstanding the friendliness of the Pearsons and other influential landowners, who desired to advantageously place him on a holding, a country life could not satisfy his aspirations or give scope to his natural qualifications. So he went to Melbourne with excellent references to Mr. Richard Gibson, of Dalmahoy Campbell & Co. This introduction led up to another coincidence, which had much to do in shaping Christie's career. It happened that Mr. Gibson required an official detective to do some private work, and, being unable to obtain one, he, after consultation with Superintendent C. H. Nicolson, offered Christie the job. It was accepted, and Christie commenced upon that use of disguises and methodical seeking of information, which afterwards he developed to such an advanced degree. The man supposed to be possessed of the facts belonged to a railway survey party, which Christie at once joined as an axeman. His adventure was entirely successful, and during the course of it he kept his straight, strong left in practice by defeating the champion of a rival camp.

Upon his return to Melbourne he was assured by Mr. Gibson that his first success as a detective would be amply rewarded and well-remembered. Shortly afterwards he defeated at "The Butchers' Arms," (kept by an ex-pugilist named George Strike), a well-known fighter known as the "Fighting Artilleryman," who had recently defeated another noted amateur, young Mr. Dal Campbell. A testimonial to Mr. Christie was subscribed by such well-known gentlemen as the Pearsons, Campbells, Messrs. Gibson, John Buncle, Hugh Lennon, etc.

## BIOGRAPHICAL INTRODUCTION.

But still Christie was without regular employment. Declining with thanks some further good offers to go on the land, he turned his eyes towards the Detective Police, whereupon Mr. Gibson gave him the following laconic note to Superintendent Nicolson, who was in charge of the Detective Office:—

"Dear Nicolson,—

"The bearer cleared up the case I spoke to you about some time ago. He is good with head and hands."

Christie was immediately sworn in and commenced his official career as a detective.

# PART I.
## AS DETECTIVE.

## Chapter I.

### INITIATION.

CHRISTIE'S first experience as a detective was uncomfortable for himself, but amusing enough to others. Indeed, it practically led to his own arrest. Certainly he had to give himself up to the police. It was in this way. When he reported himself for duty, he was ordered, raw recruit as he was, to roam the city and run down stray offenders. But he had just got to the Eastern Market, then known as Paddy's Market, only a little distance from the Detective Office, when he saw a Chinaman, the first he had ever seen. Curiosity caused him to regard the Mongolian attentively, and as he gazed the dormant detective instinct within him awoke. There was something suspicious in the man's appearance, and in his movements. So curiosity in the young detective turned to discreet watchfulness, and he unostentatiously followed the Chinaman all around town. He was rewarded, after an hour's vigil, for the man furtively approached a stall, in Paddy's Market, from which he stole two pairs of boots. Christie promptly pounced upon his prey, and placed the Chinaman under arrest. He had hooked his first fish. But now he had to land him within the net of the law, and that was not to prove as easy a task as it looked. Of course a crowd quickly gathered about the struggling couple, and when Christie had subdued his prisoner, a jeering mob followed them down the street. Unfortunately Christie, strange to Melbourne, took a wrong turn, and, instead of going straight to the Detective Office, close at hand within 30 yards, went straight away from it. He wandered far, until he encountered Police-Sergeant Summerhayes in uniform near the Carlton Gardens. This sub-officer demanded an explanation of the Chinaman, his captor, and the crowd.

"I am Detective Christie. I have arrested this man for stealing two pairs of boots, and I want to know the way to the Detective Office," explained Christie.

"Then show me your card," said the Sergeant, suspiciously, scrutinising a man who claimed to be a detective, and yet did not know the way to his own office.

Christie coloured up in confusion, for no card of authority, a most essential badge of office, had been supplied to him. He had to admit as much, whereupon the Sergeant grimly said,

"Then I'd better take both of you to the Detective Office myself."

This he did, and, of course, the laughable bungle was immediately cleared up to the satisfaction of all concerned, except the Chinaman, who was duly convicted.

Not long after this Christie was to receive another lesson. It must be remembered that at this time he was barely twenty and brimful of youthful innocence. Thus it happened that he was actually caught by some of the very magsmen whom he was sent out to catch. One of these made himself friendly with the youthful looking new-chum, and proposed a walk and then a drink. In the hotel they met two more gentlemen at large, and a game of cards was proposed. Christie fell an easy victim and lost thirty-eight shillings. He took his loss smilingly, but registered a vow to get even, for by this

## INITIATION.

time he was convinced of the shady character of his pretended friends. He left them ostensibly, but really only retired to a favourable spot from which he could view their exit and follow their movements. They soon came out, proceeded down the street, and shortly after fraternised with a gullible foreigner, whom they took for the usual drink which is the inevitable preliminary to all spielers' swindling schemes. Christie at once got two other detectives, and the hotel was watched by the three at all exits. In a little while the foreigner came out in a very excited state of mind. On being questioned he explained that he had been swindled out of his money at a game called "Cho choo chum." This was enough. The other detectives, in order that Christie's identity should remain concealed, entered the hotel and arrested the magsmen, who were in due course sentenced each to twelve months' imprisonment.

"You weren't long in getting your revenge, young fellow," said one of them subsequently, with a grin. "Why you're almost sharp enough to be one of us!"

But Christie was perfectly conscious of the fact that his so-called smartness was really only a mixture of innocence and good luck. However, he was never again either "bushed" or "taken down" in the city, with every inch of which he was destined to become familiar, from dirtiest slum to dignified Government House.

During his detective career Christie had charge of hundreds of cases, most of which ended in the arrest, conviction, and imprisonment of the criminals. His skill rapidly developed and the raw recruit matured into the erect dignified military-looking officer familiar alike to the wrongdoers and good citizens of Melbourne. At the same time his methods were more and more cultivated, until in him detection assumed almost the dignity of an art. Offenders held him in something like awe. They did not know how or when he was going to put his hand upon them. One moment a criminal would be talking affably with a polished gentleman who might be an attache of a diplomatic corps: the next he would be confronted by a stern-faced, steel-eyed Nemesis, who in a flash had presented a revolver at his head and clapped a pair of handcuffs on his wrists.

Christie's velvet glove always covered an iron hand, and in many an encounter did he find his science as a boxer stand him in good stead. This was especially so in connection with the larrikin pushes, who were at one time a menace to law-abiding men, women, and even children. One evening a group of these gentry received a very severe shock, which gave some of them, at least, a lesson sufficient to last them a lifetime. One of the detectives got Christie to arrange with Jem Mace, champion pugilist of the world, then in Australia, and another splendid fighter, to go down Russell Street and break up a notorious push which was the terror of that thoroughfare. The three pretended to be drunk, and were thus considered fair game for the gang of roughs, who commenced to jostle the seeming roysterers. But suddenly a startling sobriety took the place of staggering drunkenness. The trio, standing back to back in a triangle, dealt out blow after blow with lightning rapidity, felling their aggressors like ninepins. They inflicted very heavy punishment. That push never foregathered again. One such experience was enough, and the feeling of what fools they had been probably never left them.

## INITIATION. 23

In the work of stamping out these larrikin hordes Christie was associated with Sergeant Dalton, a noted terror to the pest and an amusing character to boot. It was he who was supposed to have originated the term "larrikin" as applied to the Apaches or Hooligans of our cities. The story goes that on charging several youths with offensive behaviour he said to the Bench in his best Irish brogue,

"Plaze yer worships, Oi found the prisoner a-larrakin' (larking) about the strates." Street ruffians have been known as larrikins throughout Australia ever since.

"How did you capture so many of them, Sergeant?" asked the magistrate, with a smile.

"Plaze, your worship, it was surrounded them moiself I did, Sorr!"

Another good story is told of Dalton in connection with what was known as Spann's robbery. It was a mysterious affair, and Mrs. Spann consulted a well-known spiritualist in the hope of getting information from the spirits. At a seance she was told that the thief would be found exactly at midnight standing beneath the Post Office clock as it struck twelve. She duly waited, and pounced upon the only man standing at the spot indicated. She seized him and was at once assailed with a wordy storm of abuse in the richest brogue that was ever produced from the bogs of the Emerald Isle. Explanations followed, and she found to her dismay that she had grappled with Sergeant Dalton! The Sergeant was ever a genial spirit, notwithstanding his gaunt appearance and rough and ready handling of larrikins. He was one of the coolest and most determined men ever in the Police Force of Victoria.

## Chapter. II.
## HALLIBURTON'S ROBBERY.

THE following is the story of a crime in which Christie is seen in some of his most characteristic phases:—

In the year 1870 a number of very daring and clever burglaries were effected in Melbourne, and the detectives were some time before they could run down the criminals. Christie was away at this time on a holiday, during which he received a telegram recalling him to duty. On reporting himself at the detective office, the Inspector in charge handed to him some crime reports which had just come in, giving an account of extensive burglaries which had been committed in two softgoods warehouses in the City. The reports showed that the operators were experts of the first rank, and had gone to work with great coolness as well as dexterity. Christie was directed to take the case in hand and use his best endeavours to arrest the thieves. His first step was to call at one of the warehouses which had been broken into, where he found the proprietor in great tribulation, having lost about £1,500 worth of goods. On examination of the premises it was evident that an entrance had been effected through the front door, the padlock on which had been broken and the door lock opened by skeleton keys.

A brief description of the means by which the burglars open a main door into a public street which is regularly patrolled by a policeman always on duty may here be deemed not uninteresting. The modus operandi is as follows:—The burglars ascertain the precise time as which the constable on the beat is relieved and the spot at which he will be met by the policeman who relieves him. At this time they anticipate that there will be an interval of ten to twenty minutes, during which they will be pretty safe in working. If there is no padlock on the door they desire to open it is soon opened by means of skeleton keys, but if there is also a padlock, as is usually the case, two of the gang will stand before the door as if conversing, whilst two others will operate on the padlock, concealed from view to a great extent by their mates who are standing in front of them. One of the men will hold a piece of stone about the size of half a brick under the padlock, which is placed on its back whilst his mate strikes it with an iron "Jimmy." As a consequence the back plate of the padlock comes off, the wards fall out, and the lock is opened. Just when the blow is about to be made the confederates commence to cough, and the slight sound occasioned by the blow would not be heard even by persons on the opposite side of the street. The broken pieces of the padlock are pitched away or concealed, the door opened, and two of the gang pass in. The two remaining outside replace the hasp and attach a padlock of the same size and make as the one broken off, and, having locked it, leave the spot, taking with them the tools used and the key of the new padlock.

This is done in very much shorter time than it takes to relate it. The burglars know that the constable on his beat tries the padlocks that are on the doors he passes, hence the necessity of replacing the broken one. The two men inside wait at the back of the door till the constable tries the padlock, leaning heavily against the door so that it may appear to the constable to be all solid and fast. As soon as he has passed, by means of their dark lanterns, they select the goods they wish to steal and carry them to the front door ready to be taken away. At the hour of the next relief the men who had gone away return with a spring cart usually containing tins of milk, drive up to the door and open the padlock. The goods ready are whipped out in an instant and placed in the cart, which is driven either to their own crib or straight to that of the "fence." The two men who had been inside being of an economical turn of mind, take off the new padlock and carry it with them, quietly strolling off as if taking an early morning walk. The constable on his next round probably discovers the robbery and the usual reports are made.

In the Halliburton case here related it was clear that not only had very clever cracksmen been at work, but that one of them must have been a very excellent judge of cloth, as the stuff taken was the best and most expensive in the warehouse. The cutter out of the establishment told Christie that one of the rolls taken had been cut by him, and, in answer to enquiry, that he had the piece cut off still by him. The piece was for a coat, and the cut was an irregular one, consequently, if the roll could be recovered the piece could be fitted in and would thus serve to identify the cloth. This would be the more fortunate because in the absence of tickets, it was usually very difficult to swear to any particular roll of cloth. The detective then proceeded to the other warehouse, which had been raided, evidently by the same gang. From this warehouse a great quantity of ready-made clothing, blankets, etc., had been taken, and which the proprietor said he would have great difficulty in identifying, but added that amongst the goods taken was a pair of shoe-brushes of a particular pattern which had on them not only his own private mark but that of the maker, and that these could be sworn to if recovered. Moreover, only six pairs of these brushes had been imported, and five were still in stock. The detective requested that these might be retained for the present.

Having reported the result of his enquiries to the Inspector and also his opinion that one of the thieves must have been a tailor, Christie then proceeded to scrutinise the list of prisoners recently discharged from gaol, paying particular attention to those described as tailors by trade, and then strolled down to a public house in Queen Street, which was a notorious haunt of criminals. On arrival, however, he found the place deserted, and, on asking the landlord where the boys were he replied that the other D.'s had been down so often lately that they had all taken the alarm and cleared out, with the exception of two or three who had taken up honest work and were now entirely "on the square." When the detective enquired who these were to whom he referred he mentioned the names of Harry Brookes and Ben Long. The first named he said was at work at his trade as a tailor, whilst the other was doing odd jobs at carpentering, and that he expected the latter down that afternoon with two forms for the bar which the landlord had ordered. The detective on hearing this, immediately returned to his quarters, where he assumed a disguise he had by him, of a swaggie or bushman, dyeing his hair, eyebrows and moustache with a preparation which would easily wash off. He then engaged a cab, into which he took his swag and, having drawn the curtains, directed the cabman to take up a position at the corner of the street which commanded the approach to the public house at which Mr. Ben Long was expected, with the result of his honest work.

After waiting a considerable time Christie at last perceived the industrious mechanic coming down the street, wheeling a hand truck in which were two forms, which he took into the hotel and then proceeded with the truck into Lonsdale Street, where he left the vehicle up a right of way. It subsequently appeared, as a reason for this singular proceeding, that he had stolen the truck from a marine store dealer, and, having served his purpose, desired to get rid of it. Having left the truck, Long jumped into a North Melbourne cab that was passing at the time. The detective followed at a respectful distance, with a view to finding out where the man lived, and feeling convinced that the honest tailor would be found in the same locality. Long left the cab in Howard Street and proceeded to a public house in that street, and as he did not emerge for some time Christie went into the place with his swag on his back and, entering the bar parlour, called for a glass of rum, which, by the way, he threw into the fire when the landlady's back was turned, and, speaking with a strong Irish brogue, invited the lady to have a nip also, to which request she graciously acceded. He then inquired if he could have a shake-down for the night, to which she replied that as he had his blankets with him, he could coil up in the shed at the back, where a couple more

Detective Christie as a Swagman.

*Facing page 28*]

J. M. Christie as a "Christy Minstrel"
at a Charity Fancy-Dress Ball.

*Facing page 29*]

were dossing down. After a little further conversation the Detective again shouted for the landlady, who, after the second glass, became very agreeable, especially when the detective told her he had recently made a rise and would like her to take care of his "sugar" for him. He then went on to tell her that he was looking for an old mate of his named "Ben the carpenter," and enquired if she knew of anyone of that name in the neighbourhood, to which she answered that a man named Ben Long, a carpenter, was living in the right-of-way behind her house, and that as his back-door opened into a yard which adjoined her own the man usually went in and out through her place. "If you leave your swag in the shed "you can go in and see if he is the mate you are looking for," added the woman; "but if you want me to take care of your money for you, you had better give it to me now or you may be robbed of it." The detective then told her to wait till he came back, as he might want some money to shout for his old mate and his missus. She told him that Ben had no missus, but had six or seven men living with him. Christie then remarked that if he had no missus he was not the man he was seeking and, picking up his swag, went to the shed in the yard, where he placed it and then took a look round at the locality.

He saw that there were only two cottages in the right-of-way. The window of one was covered up with calico and the yard very untidy and dirty. At the door of the other, which though a wretched hovel was yet very clean and tidy, an old woman was sitting in the doorstep with several children playing about. Lighting his pipe, Christie strolled over to her and enquired of her who lived next door, as he might get the job of doing up the yard. She replied that she did not know, but that whoever they were, they were not of much account, as they slept all day and only went out after dark, and on returning brought with them big bags full of stuff, which she could hear them dump on the floor. She added that one morning her husband, on getting up, had found that some one had been using his horse and spring cart, which he had cleaned over night and then found very dirty, and found wheel marks leading to the door of the next cottage, and that her husband was going to put the police on to the neighbours.

When Christie heard this he was satisfied he was on the right track and, bidding the woman good day, he passed back through the hotel out into the street and picked up his cab where he had left it standing. Giving the cabbie a nod to follow, he walked into the next street; there he jumped in and drove off at once to the detective office, where Detectives Brown and Harrington were picked up. Proceeding thence to his quarters, Christie resumed his usual attire. The party then proceeded to the public house where Christie's swag had been left, and whilst the latter engaged the landlady in conversation Detective Brown slipped through unperceived, as previously agreed on between the detectives, into the shed.

Here he was joined by Christie, and the two then slipped into Long's back yard and crept up to the door, the keyhole of which was plugged up with paper. Christie pushed the plug quietly out with his knife, and, on looking through, saw Long and two other men in the front measuring and cutting up cloth. On seeing this, leaving Brown to watch the back door, Christie hurried back to the cab and, telling Harrington to follow, proceeded round to Long's front door, which he tried, but finding it locked, taking care to keep out of sight of the window, he knocked gently and heard some one inside say "Who is there?" To which the detective replied in a low voice, "It's me, Ben." The door was then opened slightly, when Harrington and Christie dashed at it and, getting inside, Harrington locked it and then turned to help his brother officer, who was engaged in a desperate struggle with the three men who had all fallen on him at once. The fight lasted for some time, and was a pretty rough one while it lasted, but in the end the three men were handcuffed and secured. Brown was then admitted by the back door, through the keyhole of which he had been gazing at the encounter, without however being able to come to his fellow detectives' assistance.

The three men taken were Long, Brookes and Thomas alias "Jack the Lagger," but it was hoped the rest of the gang might be secured. With this object in view the three captives were made to sit down on the floor in the back room, whilst Christie took a chair, sitting down behind the front door, determined to await the arrival of the other men who formed the rest of the gang. He had not been there long when a knock came at the door, which was opened by the detective, who kept well behind it, when two men stepped into the room, which was unlighted. Christie slammed the door to and locked it, and before the new arrivals could realize that they were trapped, they were handcuffed and placed with the others in the back room, after a bit of a struggle. The last comers were Baker (alias Young), and Edwards (alias Brown). Not content with the haul already made, and judging from what the landlady had said as to the number of men living at Ben Long's, it was determined to see if any more would turn up, accordingly the door of the room in which the men were caged being closed.

Christie resumed his position behind the front door. His patience was soon rewarded, for after a short interval there was another knock, and in a low voice the detective asked who was there, when a voice replied, "It's all right, Ben." On the door being opened a man and woman stepped in and the door was at once locked and Christie called for a light, which being brought disclosed the fact that they had netted two more notorious criminals—McEwan and "Mother" Waddle, each having aliases. The new comers joined the happy party, and as the supply of handcuffs had run short they were made fast with a clothes line found on the premises. Having the thieves secure, a boy outside was sent for the cab which had been waiting all the time (the driver being a man usually employed by Christie on his pleasant jaunts), and was on arrival sent to the Police Station for three constables, and to bring two furniture vans to remove the stolen goods with which the place was crowded. On arrival of the reinforcement, the prisoners were bundled into the cab and the plunder placed in the vans and all taken to the detective office, where the other detectives were found all sitting at muster.

The arrival of seven prisoners and two van loads of recovered property created considerable excitement and jubilation, as such a large haul at once seldom occurs. The prisoners were all placed in the lock up pending their trial. The next day Christie returned to Howard Street, where he found the inhabitants much excited over the night's happenings. He called at the hotel which he had previously visited in disguise and told the landlady whom he had thought he had captivated the day before, that one of the party who had been arrested was at her hotel the day before and had left his swag in the shed. She replied: "Do you mean the red-headed man?" and being answered in the affirmative said: "Oh the man was a thief, and I would not let him sleep in the house. He had a lot of money, and the scamp wanted me to take care of it for him, but as I thought it was crooked I would have nothing to do with it." When Christie told her he was the red-headed man and thus knew exactly what had passed between them she became very abusive, and the detective, after obtaining his swag, left. He then called on the old woman who lived next door to Long's and who was much pleased at the clearing out of the gang. He next inspected Long's premises, and there found the marked shoe brushes which had been overlooked before, and under the hearthstone a jimmy, skeleton keys, a loaded revolver, a dark lantern, and a large brass padlock, which had evidently been the one used in the robbery. Pieces of the tickets which had been on the cloth were found half burnt in the fireplace. On examination of the cloth recovered the roll from which the piece had been cut was found intact, and the two fitted exactly. The gang was duly tried and convicted and sentenced each to eight years' imprisonment with hard labour. The detectives were highly complimented by the presiding judge on the ability shown in the conduct of the cases. Christie himself was presented with amounts totalling twenty-five pounds in recognition of his part in the case.

At the trial Aspinall, the celebrated barrister and wit, defended the prisoners and attempted to discredit Christie's statement that he had viewed the interior of the thieves' den through a keyhole.

"Supposing I bring the landlord to prove that the door has no keyhole, what would you say?" he asked.

"That I looked through a keyhole," replied Christie.

But the judge was obviously impressed by the apparent earnestness of the barrister, and directed Christie and another officer to proceed and further examine the door.

"Does your Honour expect them to bring back the keyhole?" asked Aspinall to the amusement of all.

They did, however, bring back the next best thing. That was a piece of wood with which the keyhole had been plugged up.

That settled the case. A verdict of guilty was brought in, and the eight offenders all received heavy sentences, as stated.

## Chapter III.
### ROBBERIES.

ONE Sunday night, the warehouse of Haigh Bros., a firm of tailors situated in Collins Street, was broken into by burglars, who had effected entrance through the roof by breaking in a skylight, and by the aid of a rope ladder. The thieves carried off property valued at several hundred pounds, and one of the partners on Monday morning immediately reported the matter to the detective office. Detectives Williams and Christie were told off at once to take the case in hand. The two officers had no difficulty in soon seeing that expert cracksmen had been at work. The officers arranged to meet at the post office at 8 in the evening.

Christie dressed himself up to give himself the appearance of a bushman just arrived from the back country, sauntered down to the post office and waited for his brother detective. Whilst seated he was spied by a constable, who went up to him and told him to move on. Christie, saying nothing, got up and strolled along through the crowd at the corner of the street, and whilst so doing the same constable again noticed him and, walking up to him, said, "If you do not clear out of this at once I'll "vag" you, as I know you are a magsman." At this particular moment Christie's mate came on the scene and, having seen his disguise before, recognised him but said nothing. Christie then sauntered away into Little Bourke Street, and was soon followed by Williams, who joined him, telling him as a great joke that the constable who had told Christie to clear out had just informed him that the latter was a notorious magsman and a card sharper named Murphy. Williams, hardly able to keep his countenance, had said that he would shepherd Murphy and went after the supposed magsman.

Whilst the two detectives were standing in front of an hotel a man passed whom Christie had seen discharged from Pentridge Prison about three weeks before, named William Owen. On seeing this man he said to Williams, "Why there goes Owen who was discharged only the other day. I wonder what he is up to now?" Williams replied, "If that is Bill Owen you may be sure he was on the job we have in hand, because he is an expert cracksman, and being moreover a tailor by calling, would be the most likely man to be concerned in a robbery of cloth and mercery." Christie parted with Williams and followed Owen up the street as far as the entrance to the Theatre Royal, where Owen met another man apparently by appointment, and, having purchased tickets, both men went into the pit of the Theatre. Christie followed the two men and sat down on a seat immediately behind them. Between the acts they conversed in very low and generally inaudible tones together, but from a few fragments of their conversation, Christie felt sure he was on the right track and that they were the men who were wanted. Owen was heard to say to his friend that as they had a large swag of silk handkerchiefs on hand, they had better get rid of them, and that he thought he could fence them with old Levi, who was a notorious fence, and that the latter could "stand for them."

Owen, at the conclusion of the play, left with his mate and they walked up Bourke Street together, but parted company opposite Parliament House, Owen telling his mate to be sure and be up early in the morning, to which the latter replied, "All right." The detective followed Owen through various streets to a cottage in Victoria Street, which the man entered, and soon after his entrance a light was seen in one of the windows, which Christie concluded was Owen's room. He noticed a card in the window, on which was printed "William Jones, Tailor." On enquiring at a neighbouring hotel of the landlord the officer was informed that the owner of the cottage was a decent old man who let two rooms furnished to lodgers, but the names of the latter were not known.

On returning to the cottage, the detective having entered the garden, crawled up to the window in which the light was seen, and, looking under the corner of the blind, could make out a man undressing, who got to bed and blew out the candle. Seeing his quarry apparently disposed of for the night, Christie hailed a passing cab and, jumping in, ordered the cabman to drive to Williams' house. Having roused up the detective, the two returned to Owen's house, which they intended to search. On arrival, Christie knocked at the window, and an old man came with a light. The detective motioned him to open the front door, and Christie having told his business, went into the old man's bedroom.

The old man told all that he knew of his lodger. He said that on Sunday evening, the night of the robbery, Owen had gone out and did not return till nearly daylight, and that as Owen had forgotten to take his latch key with him, he had to get up and let him in. His lodger had two other men with him, and had come in a cab, from which they carried several bundles into Owen's room. The mates then drove away. His lodger told the old man that he had brought some goods there to start tailoring.

Detective Christie then went to the door of Owen's room, entered noiselessly, and found the occupant fast asleep. Lighting a candle he held it to the sleeper's face, at the same time shaking him by the shoulder. The sleeper, starting up, said, "Hallo, what's up?" "It is all right, Bill," said Christie. "I am a detective, and am going to search your rooms for goods stolen from that warehouse in Collins Street that you cracked on Sunday night." "Who gave me away?" said the man, "for you seem to know all about it." "Never mind," said the officer. "Get up and dress yourself." Then, calling to Williams to come, they arrested the man and slipped the handcuffs on him. Searching the room, they found about £150 worth of goods in the room, some of which were marked with the name of the firm from which they had been stolen. Christie then asked the landlord if he could describe and identify the two men that came with Owen when the packages were brought to the house, and obtained from him a full description of them. From this he found the description given of one of the men was identical with that of the man he had seen in Owen's company at the Theatre, and accordingly the detective determined to await the man's arrival. About nine o'clock a knock was heard, and the landlord said that it was one of the men he had seen previously.

Christie told him to tell the caller that Owen had gone out.

The man then went away, followed by Christie to a small cottage in Collingwood. Christie drove to Detective Williams' house, and the two officers returned to the cottage. Williams having established himself at the back door, Christie knocked at the front and, receiving no answer, burst it open. He found the cottage was entirely empty. While the detectives were then discussing what they should do next, one of the persons in the neighbourhood, a female who had been attracted to the spot by the noise made in breaking open the door, told them the house was hers, and that two men had rented it from her a few days before, and although they had paid the rent in advance had not yet taken up their abode there, though they had been several times in and out. Her son informed them also that on Monday morning early he had seen the men come in a cab and take several bundles from it, which they had carried into the house. They had then subsequently carried the bundles out through the back yard to another cab. On asking the boy if he could recognise the cabman if he saw him, the sharp lad replied, "You bet I would." Christie took the boy and drove round to the different cab stands in the neighbourhood to try and spot the cabman they wanted. The youngster was promised a half-sovereign if he could pick out the man. After driving about for a little time the boy called out, "There he is," indicating a cabman who was passing, having his vehicle loaded up with passengers and luggage. This man was hailed and the position explained to him, and arrangement was made by which his load was transferred to the detectives' cab, whilst the latter got into the second cab. The driver said he perfectly remembered the occurrence of driving the men and bundles on Monday morning, and could take them straight to the place where he had driven them.

Leaving the cab in a right-of-way close to the building, the two detectives effected an entrance through one of the windows. They found no one inside, but found the rest of the goods which had been stolen from the tailor's in Collins Street. The officers then sat down to await the return of the men. Very soon footsteps were heard on the front verandah, and the two men walked in. Christie came out, and, on seeing him, one of the men said, "Oh, I see, we have made a mistake. I beg pardon; we have come into the wrong house. Having just taken a place, we did not know it very well," and the men turned to go away. To this the officer replied genially, "Oh, you need not apologise, my friend. You have made no mistake. We are very glad to see you, and you are very welcome."

Before they could recover themselves Williams and Christie had indicated the nature of the welcome which was extended them by deftly slipping the handcuffs on both of them and telling them they were prisoners. The cabman was then called in, and fully identified the men and also the bundles. The men were found to be actually wearing suits with the name of the firm they had been stolen from on them, and in the oven of the kitchen range was found a complete kit of burglars' tools, including skeleton keys of all kinds and a "jimmy" known as an alderman in the profession. This implement was a clever piece of workmanship and ingenuity, and, by its means, if a key had been left in the lock of a door on the inside, the door could be readily and noiselessly unlocked from the outside. In addition was also found a beautifully made rope ladder, soft and pliable and yet very strong, which could be carried easily round the body secure from observation. On the jaws of the "alderman" being compared with the marks of the skylight on the building, they were found to fit exactly. The two burglars were convicted and each sentenced to five years' imprisonment with hard labour.

CHAPTER IV.

## BROOKS AND WILSON, COINERS.

TOWARDS the end of the year 1869, an immense number of counterfeit coins were in circulation, principally half-crowns and florins, and they were so well made that it was only when they were tendered to the banks that the deception was discovered.

The manager of the Bank of Victoria sent for Christie, and showed him some of the counterfeits. Having received the addresses of some of the persons who had been victimised, the detective called on them, but the only clue he could get was that all of them suspected a medium-sized man, who always had a little fair-haired girl, about five or six years old, with him. He then carefully went through the descriptions of prisoners recently discharged from Pentridge, who had undergone sentences for coining. He could only find three—Robert Smith, Joseph Brooks, and John Wilson.

Smith, previous to his last sentence, lived in Synagogue Lane with a woman named Lizzie Ferguson. Christie dropped into her old haunts, armed with a search warrant, and, accompanied by Detective Hudson, knocked at the door, calling out, "Milk-oh!"

Lizzie, seeing it was Christie, said, "You're a nice milkman. What's up?"

Christie said, "Is Bob in?" and she replied that he was.

## BROOKS AND WILSON, COINERS. 43

Bob was just turning out, and was greeted with, "Well, Bob, I have come to look for a red thimble and slang (gold watch and chain) that was pinched last night."

He replied, "Well now, Christie, I'm surprised at you. I'm only out a few weeks, and have turned square."

Christie asked him where he was working, and he replied, "I have been doing a few odd jobs among the boats down at the river, and besides the old woman has a quid or two in the Savings Bank."

After a fruitless search for a coining plant the detective casually remarked:—"By the bye, I see Joe Brooks and his mate, Jack Wilson, are out."

Bob replied, "Yes, they came out after me. I was up in the Market with my old woman Saturday night, and we met Joe with his little girl."

I said, "How old is the girl? I did not know he had one."

He replied, "Oh yes; she's a pretty little fair-haired child about five years old, and the image of his old woman."

I asked what had become of the "old woman."

"She got a couple of stretch (years) for snowdropping (robbing clothes lines), and she's done about half of her time."

I said, "Well, who looks after the girl?"

He replied, "Joe does. He seemed flush of cash and shouted several times for us at the Adam and Eve. He said he was working on the square at a timber yard in Rokeby Street, Collingwood."

Christie went home and donned his old labourer's suit, and dropped down by a Simpson's Road cab to Rokeby

Street, but could find no timber yard, so he strolled up to the Glasshouse Hotel, the landlord of which he knew. Christie disclosed his identity to him, and told him what he was after, giving a description of Brooks and his little girl.

He replied, "Well, I believe I know the man you mean. He lives in a small sort of courtyard about two hundred yards down Rokeby Street on the opposite side from here. Come outside and I'll show you."

Christie replied, "Not just now. We'll wait till dark, and then you can show me."

"Well, come upstairs and I'll show you the entrance to the yard from the street from one of my bedroom windows," and from the upstairs window we had a splendid view.

The detective determined to wait till dark and then reconnoitre the courtyard. Towards dusk, up came the landlord and said, "The man I mean is in the bar having a drink with a man who's often with him."

Christie went down into the private bar-parlor, and got a splendid view of them through the glass door leading into the bar. They were Joe Brooks and John Wilson.

When it got dark Christie strolled down the street and into the yard. There were three small cottages, containing two rooms each, with doors opening into the yard. The top one had a notice up, "Mangling Done Here." He went up to the house. The door was open, and a fat little jolly sort of woman was sitting in front of the fire. He said to her, "Can you tell me which house black Johnson lives in?" and she replied, "Well, there's no niggers living in this street."

He said, "Well, he gave me directions to come here," and she told him that at the end house of the three there was a charwoman, and in the centre one there were two men and a little girl.

Almost as she spoke, out came the child with a jug and ran off to the hotel for a jug of beer. She was just the sort of girl described to Christie by the persons who had been victimised with the base coins. The mangle woman said, "There is something queer going on next door. They never get up till 10 or 11 o'clock in the forenoon. They always keep their door locked, and sometimes there is a great smell of chemicals."

Christie said, "These are very small cottages," and she replied, "Yes; I pay 6/- a week rent, and there is no back yard, only a door leading out to the front." That was satisfactory, thought the detective, as there was no get-away at the back.

Obtaining a search warrant, Christie, with Detective Hudson, proceeded next forenoon about 10 o'clock to the house. They were dressed in their ordinary clothes, and crept up the yard past Brooks' window on their hands and knees. They could hear those in the cottage working at something; it sounded like pegging boots. They burst in the door, and discovered Brooks and Wilson in the very act of coining.

Brooks had a ladle full of metal in his hand, and made a hit at Christie, who floored him with a left-hander and got the handcuffs on him. In the meantime Wilson had thrown Hudson and sprung through the window, taking sash and all with him. Leaving Brooks with Hudson, Christie chased Wilson, caught and threw him, holding him down till Driver-Detective Kidney came up.

Searching the house, the detectives found all the appliances requisite for coining, including dies, battery, chemicals, &c. The coins they had just made were still hot and of the same year as those Christie had seen at the Bank of Victoria. They also found a quantity of the metal used in manufacturing the coins.

The two men were in due course committed for trial, and at the criminal sittings of the Supreme Court, on the 15th December, 1869, they were tried, found guilty, and sentenced to four years hard labour each. The little girl, charged as a neglected child, was sent up to gaol to her mother, who had some months still to serve.

## Chapter V.

### O'GRADY'S ROBBERY.

DURING the night of the 5th March, 1870, the dwelling of Mr. Michael O'Grady, at Hawthorn, was broken into by burglars. Amongst the stolen property there was a magnificent silver centre stand of the value of 200 guineas. Christie was directed to take up the case, and he came to the conclusion that the robbery was the work of two desperate young burglars named George Lindley and Robert Bitson, who lived with their paramours in a lane off Little Lonsdale Street.

Christie rigged himself out in a dilapidated old suit and wideawake hat, put one arm in a sling and a bandage round his head, and took up a position commanding the entrance to the right of way in which they all lived.

Just at dusk, Lindley came out and went into the corner hotel, followed in a few minutes by Bitson, better known as "White-headed Bob." When they came out they proceeded into Madeline Street, and came to a barber's shop with the name of John Manix over the door.

About ten months previously Manix, who had occupied the position of barber in Pentridge Stockade off and on during the previous nineteen years—nearly the whole of which time he had been in the Stockade for daring crimes—had been discharged from Pentridge. He enlisted the sympathy of an old and respected clergyman of Carlton, and induced him to set him up in the shop.

Christie walked boldly into the shop and, sitting down on a chair, desired to be shaved. He saw at once that Manix was identical with the ex-Pentridge barber, and sitting on a form were Lindley and Bitson in close conversation. After being shaved, Christie engaged a cab, put down the curtains, and pulled up in view of Manix's shop. After some little time Lindley and Bitson came out and returned to their respective "drums."

Next day Christie watched the whole of the day from a shop nearly opposite. Nearly every night the three met, generally about 9 o'clock in the evening, when they would lock the front door and put the blind down.

One evening, when they were all locked in, Christie ventured up to Manix's back gate. He could hear the three men talking inside the house. He listened attentively, and presently saw Manix come outside into his yard and bury something. He also threw some hot ashes out. In a little time Lindley and Bitson came out, and Christie heard Manix say to them, "Well, come up to-morrow evening, and we'll whack up."

Early next morning Christie was at his friend's shop in Madeline Street, to watch Manix. During the day he came out and walked down to a pawn office. After a few minutes, he came out and went back up Swanston Street. Christie went into the shop and said to the pawnbroker, "What did that man want?" He replied, "I was just going to send up for you, as there is something suspicious about him. He told me he was a working jeweller, and wanted to sell me this piece of melted up silver, weighing 90ozs. I told him to leave it with me

Detective Christie watching a Suspected Dwelling.

Facing page 48]

while I tested it, and he could return in a couple of hours for the money." The silver was evidently part of O'Grady's centre stand melted down.

Christie placed Detective Daly in the pawn shop, to hear any conversation that might ensue on Manix's return, but he injudiciously showed himself, and Manix ran out of the shop. Seeing Manix making off up Swanston Street in a cab, Christie drove quickly to the pawn office, picked up Detective Daly, and started in hot pursuit. Getting to Franklyn Street, the detectives had overhauled Manix's cab. The two collided, and the officers were thrown out. Manix ran for the right-of-way at the back of his shop, where Christie caught him. He fought desperately, but Christie knocked him down and handcuffed him, took the key of his front shop door out of his pocket, and Daly and he brought Manix into his shop.

They searched the place, and found the whole of the silver centre stand in different pieces, except some portions which had been melted up into the block he had offered for sale. Other portions of the stand, silver figures, were found in various parts of the roof, hid amongst the rafters. In the yard, partly covered up, was found a splendid new crucible, which had apparently been only used once or twice. In a small shed was a small bag of charcoal, some borax, and a pair of bellows, all useful and necessary for melting down metal.

Warrants were obtained for the arrest of Lindley and Bitson, charged with burglary at O'Grady's house. In a few nights the three offenders were arrested, and in due course each sentenced to five years hard labour.

## CHAPTER VI.

### CATCHING A FORGER.

DURING the year 1871 Christie was on the lookout for a forger from New South Wales, and his whereabouts were supposed to be known to a Mr. Kato, a cattle drover, who lived at McKenzie's boarding house, where Christie also put up. During his sojourn there he made the acquaintance of Mr. Alexander Rose, manager of the National Bank at Emerald Hill (South Melbourne). They became great chums. Through him Christie succeeded in tracing Fraser, the suspected forger, to Tumut. Fraser was arrested, tried, and convicted of forgery, and received a sentence of five years.

At this time Rose knew Christie was a detective. After three or four months of Rose's acquaintance, it struck Christie that he lived greatly in excess of his income. He seemed particularly anxious to impress upon Christie that he had large interests in some of the best mines at Sandhurst (Bendigo), particularly the Great Extended Hustlers. His detective instinct caused Christie to ascertain the truth of the matter, and enquiry proved that no person named Rose held shares in any Bendigo mine. The bank was the mine that was being bled. Rose was engaged to one of the handsome daughters of a popular butcher at Emerald Hill, and he had been very lavish in his presents. The marriage day was fixed.

## CATCHING A FORGER.

One morning Christie accompanied him on his way to the bank, and said to him, "Do you wish to sell any of your shares in the Hustlers?" He coloured up, and said, "Certainly not. Why?"

Looking him straight in the face, Christie said, "Rose, you must think I am a fool not to tumble to your little game; you have not a single share in the Hustlers, and I may tell you straight, after the lies you have told me I can come to no other conclusion than that you are robbing the bank." He seemed as if struck dumb, but recovering his self-possession, said, "I will make you pay dearly for what you have said," and, turning on his heel, walked quickly away.

During the next day information came to the Detective Office that Rose was missing. A detective was told off, and the auditors soon found out several cases of embezzlement against him. Previous to leaving Melbourne, he wrote letters purporting to be from the manager of the branch of the National Bank at Prahran to the managers of the branches at Learmonth and Buninyong, advising each of them that drafts had been issued on them for £200 (each) in favour of George Leslie. He rode to Learmonth, entered the bank, and enquired if £200 had been forwarded to him, and being answered in the affirmative, the money was duly handed over. He then rode to Buninyong, where he repeated the same tactics, and received another £200. He then proceeded to Ballarat, and on the way, in case of accidents, he cut the telegraph wires.

He determined to avoid Ballarat and go to Bendigo, where he remained that night, and an early start next morning took him to Murchison, where he saw the Melbourne papers containing an account of his misdeeds, his full description, and an intimation that a reward of £50 was guaranteed for his arrest and conviction. This scared him very much, and he decided to give himself up. He sat down and wrote the following letter to Christie:—

Murchison.

Dear Christie,—

Meet me at the Shamrock Hotel, Sandhurst, at 8 p.m., on the 3rd, and you can earn £50. I am bound to be caught, and would sooner you get the reward than anyone else.

I remain yours sincerely,<br>ALEX. ROSE.

But he changed his mind before posting the letter, and decided to try to escape to New South Wales. He rode to Violet Town, where he put up for the night at the leading hotel. The hotel-keeper was a farmer, and owned a number of sheep, and was generally considered a good judge of mutton. He asked Rose how he liked the country, and Rose replied, "I will have to like it. I am the newly-appointed Government Inspector of scab in sheep."

"Oh," replied the publican, "I am pleased to make your acquaintance. If you come out to the back I will show you some fine sheep. He soon found that Rose knew nothing whatever about sheep, and decided that he was an impostor. He went straight off to the Police Station to inform the officer in charge.

When the Senior Constable called at the hotel Rose was at dinner. He and the publican went into Rose's bedroom, and there the police officer saw some pieces of paper in the fireplace. He picked them up, and put them in his pocket, tore up another piece to resemble the others, and left them in the fireplace. He then went into a private parlour, put the pieces of paper together, and found it was the letter Rose had written to Christie. The senior constable then promptly arrested Rose, and on searching him £370 in gold was found. He was subsequently tried, found guilty, and sentenced to four years' imprisonment. The Senior Constable got the reward, and he had a good laugh at Christie over it.

## CHAPTER VII.
## AN OPERA SINGER'S JEWELS.

CHRISTIE'S prestige as a detective was often the cause of his being approached privately to render service in the detection of mysterious crimes. A notable instance of this was what was known as the Lyster Robbery in 1874. It was a matter of burglary, in which the residence of Mr. William Saurin Lyster, the well-known grand opera entrepreneur of the seventies, had been broken into. A haul of jewellery to the value of £350, mostly presents made to Mrs. Lyster, had been secured. From the beginning the detectives were completely baffled, and, in spite of the incentive of a £50 reward offered by Mr. Lyster, they got more and more at sea as their inquiries proceeded. At last Mr. Lyster lost all patience, and wrote to the press, commenting severely upon the incompetency of the police. His grievance was that the detectives, while assuming most mysterious airs, never got any nearer the elucidation of the crime, the arrest of the criminal, or the recovery of the property. Instead, they continued to flounder in a tangle of "theories." First, they sagely ascribed the crime to professional expert thieves; then they thought that possibly some inmate of the house was the culprit; next, they hazarded the notion that the job might have been the work of some tradesman, visiting or employed about the house. These wild speculations exasperated Mr. Lyster, because he was quite satisfied that they were absurd. He knew, for instance, that no inmate of the house could have been the thief, because on the night

## AN OPERA SINGER'S JEWELS.

of the burglary only himself, Mrs. Lyster, and a trusted servant, who, moreover, slept with Mrs. Lyster, occupied the premises. The tradesman theory was equally preposterous. So in desperation Mr. Lyster called upon Christie. The rest of the story is best told in Christie's own words:—

I promised to do my utmost to run the thieves down, and Lyster said, "Business is business; here is £10; spare no expense." I replied, "No thanks, Mr. Lyster; you have already generously offered £50. If I succeed that will recompense me."

The result of my examination merely showed me that the robbery had been executed by men who thoroughly understood their work, and had left not the slightest clue behind them. I determined to hunt up all the professional cracksmen and see what they were all up to. In a few days after this, as I was passing down Bourke Street opposite Paddy's Market, I spotted an old friend of mine, Dick Jones, the tailor, only recently discharged from Pentridge, after doing a sentence for the robbery at Haigh Bros. I hailed him with, "Hullo, Dick! You are getting very proud." He replied, "Well, Christie, I did not know you at first." Then I said, "You had a hand in that robbery at Lyster's the other night"; and he replied, "That is the first I heard of Lyster's job." I said, "That is all rot. You and your mates did it, sure enough"; and he replied, "No, Christie; you're on the wrong lay this time." I said, "The swag consisted of jewellery, and there is £50 reward; if you put me on I'll give you £25." "A 'fence' wouldn't give much for the stuff, as it is only fit for the melting-pot," Dick replied. "If I had the swag, I wouldn't know what to do with it, as I don't know a 'fence' in the town."

I now determined to lay a plot for him. I told him the names of two pawnbrokers—Henry Scott, of Stephen Street, and William James, of Bourke Street. The first was the crookedest "fence" in Melbourne, and the latter was the honestest man in his business.

I said to Jones, "Now, old man, £25 if you put me on to the job." He replied, "Now, Christie, you ought to know me better than to think I would split on a mate." I said, "Well, I'll have both the men and the stuff before many days are over. The only thing I'm frightened of is that the swag will be taken to Harry Scott's in Stephen Street, or to old James's at the top of Bourke Street. If it is, it will be in the melting-pot in less than five minutes after." He said, "I always thought old James was a square head"; and I replied, "He stands for any quantity of stuff and melts it down at once; that's why we can't get on to him."

Dick left me, and after he had gone a short distance I hailed a cab and followed him at a distance, till I saw him go into a house in Levison Street, Hotham. In one of the front windows was hung a card, with "R. Jones, Tailor," printed on it. I returned in the cab to Melbourne and drove straight to James the pawnbroker's, to whom I said, "Now, James, I want you to help me. You have a list of the jewellery stolen from Lyster's, have you not?" He replied, "Yes," and I said, "Well, I met a notorious burglar this morning, who was likely to have had a hand in Lyster's robbery, and he told me if he had the swag he would not know where to sell it, so I told him that you and Harry Scott were the crookedest and worst fences in Melbourne."

Mr. James thanked me for giving him such a good character, and I said, "Now, if he has had a hand in the robbery and comes with anything suspicious, I want you to buy it and send for me at once. Come and I'll show you where I can be found when not at the Detective Office. I have rented a shop; the front window looks straight into Scott's pawnshop, which I am going to watch closely."

James promised to act up to my instructions. I then acquainted Inspector Secretan of what I had done, and obtained a special detective to assist me. I then proceeded to my hotel and rigged myself up like a swagman. We went to my shop in Stephen Street and whitewashed the front window, leaving a small streak, out of which we could watch without being seen.

That day we saw nothing, but returned to our posts at 7 o'clock next morning, before Scott opened his shop. At about 1 o'clock we heard a knock at the back door. I slipped down the passage and peeped through a side window, and saw that it was old James, the pawnbroker.

He said, "I think I have got something in your line," and pulled out of his pocket a piece of newspaper. It contained some loose diamonds. He said, "This lozenge-shaped stone answers the description of one of the ring stones in Lyster's robbery; it has a peculiar flaw in it, and they may be able to identify the stone. If they can, I can give you a good clue. I purchased the diamonds from a man for £20, and I gave him £10 on account. I told him that was all the money I had in the shop, and to come back for the balance next day. If you have any more I will buy them."

"He said, 'I have no more stones, but I have a little jewellery I may bring and sell to you.'"

I examined the piece of paper the stones were wrapped up in, and said, "Did the man give you the stones in this piece of paper?"

James said, "No; the piece he had them wrapped up in was a dirty piece of newspaper. I threw it into the waste paper basket."

I said, "We must go to your shop and get it. I want to examine it."

We found the piece of newspaper. It had been a part of the *Herald,* and had a part of an address still on it—

nes,

on St.,

tham.

I put the piece of paper carefully away, and James described the man. His description tallied exactly with Jones. I hunted up the *Herald* of the same day; it contained a full account of Lyster's robbery, and had evidently been sent to Jones by some of his pals on that account. I drove to the Opera House to see Lyster, who asked me if I had had any luck.

I replied, "I think so, if you can identify any of these stones;" to which he replied, "I could not, but Mrs. Lyster can," and he sent for her. She picked out the lozenge-shaped stone at once, as being a stone out of one of her rings.

Obtaining a cab, and the assistance of Detective Hartney, I at once proceeded to Jones's house. Hartney went to the back, and I knocked at the front door, which was opened by Jones himself. He staggered back on seeing me. I said, "Hullo, Dick, what's up? You

## AN OPERA SINGER'S JEWELS.

look ill," and he replied, "What do you want here?"

I said, "I hear you have some skeleton keys which you brought from Pentridge with you when you were discharged. You got them made in the blacksmith's shop by Levi Walker, and there is a row about it, so I want them."

He replied, "I have none, and, if I had, I wouldn't be such a mug as to keep them in my drum." "Well," I continued, "I must search and see."

We thoroughly searched the house and yard, but found nothing. We walked down to Victoria Street, and on getting round the corner, I told my cabman to wait about the corner and keep an eye on Jones's house, and that if he came out to try and follow him, unless he engaged him; if so, as soon as he was paid off to come to my hotel at once.

Hartney and I were just finishing dinner when my cabman came rushing in out of breath, and said to me, "Shortly after you left, Jones came quickly down the street towards me, and said, 'I want you. Drive down to King Street.' I drove on down, and when we got to the corner of the Flagstaff Gardens he jumped out, went into the gardens by the corner entrance, and returned with something concealed under his waistcoat. He then told me to drive to the Adam and Eve Hotel in Little Collins Street, and on getting there he slipped round the corner into the small lane leading into Collins Street, then doubled into a small right-of-way, and went into the back entrance to Scott's Pawn Office." I asked him how long it was since he went into the yard, and he replied not five minutes.

Hartney and I jumped into the cab and drove to

Scott's. Hartney went to the back, and I walked into the shop by the front door. When Scott came out, I said to him, "Has any one been here offering you any jewellery for sale?" and he replied, "There is a man inside now who has a lot of jewellery for sale. He is showing it to my wife."

I rushed in and there was Dick Jones with a paper parcel full of jewellery on his knees showing it to Mrs. Scott. He was completely staggered. I asked Mrs. Scott who the jewellery belonged to, and she replied, pointing to Jones, "That man has just brought it here for sale." Turning to Jones, I said, "I told you, Dick, I would get the jewellery, in spite of you."

He made no answer, and I called Hartney in, took possession of the jewellery, and removed Jones to the Dectective Office, and we locked him up in the watch-house, charged with burglary.

The same evening I took the jewellery to the Opera House and Lyster identified it at once as his. It was intact except that the stones were taken out. We saw the ring in which the lozenge-shaped stone had been; we tried it in, and it fitted exactly. I then observed that the newspaper in which the jewellery was wrapped was the *Herald*. I got the piece in which the diamonds were packed, and on examining the two, the small piece fitted exactly into the large piece. Moreover, the large piece had the other part of the address previously referred to. The case was now complete."

Jones was brought up at the City Court, committed for trial, and at the Supreme Court on November 15, 1874, he was found guilty, and sentenced to five years' hard labor.

Mr. Lyster immediately handed me the reward he had offered, viz., £50, and a complimentary ticket to admit two to any theatre under his control as long as he was in the business.

## CHAPTER VIII.
### THE "SNOWBIRD" CASE.

SOME years ago, the bankruptcy of a large firm of merchants in Sydney caused considerable stir in commercial circles, and the facts which subsequently came to light in connection with the affair were somewhat remarkable. The partners having got into pecuniary difficulties determined to work a swindle in order to raise sufficient money to enable them to carry on until the marriage of one of them to a wealthy heiress, which had been arranged, would enable them to make use of her fortune to set themselves on their feet and wipe off their liabilities. The scheme they hit upon was to purchase goods largely, then ostensibly ship them by their own vessel to some other port, and then cause the ship which carried them to be lost. They intended to insure heavily, and expected to be able to obtain the insurance money promptly, and, having obtained the goods originally on long bills, would be able to make use of the money in the interval. But this was not all. Instead of exporting the actual goods, they intended to ship dummy cases only, with the same marks on them.

In pursuance of the scheme determined on, the firm purchased the schooner *Snowbird* and loaded her with a dummy cargo. They had appointed a master, who was also in the swindle, and the ship was duly cleared by him at the Customs for Sweers Island, in the Gulf of Carpentaria. The fictitious cargo was insured for £10,000 and the vessel for her value only.

No doubt the swindlers thought it safer not to overinsure the ship, as to have done so would have caused enquiry and investigation when she was lost. When on the voyage and about 60 miles from Cleveland Bay in Queensland, the ship took fire and was burnt, the master and crew taking to the boats and arriving safely at that port. In connection with this matter, it was a somewhat significant fact that a barque owned by the same firm about the same time left Auckland and was never more heard of.

Meanwhile the goods ostensibly shipped in the *Snowbird* were being disposed of by the partners, and a portion of them was sent to Melbourne to be sold. On account of pressure of creditors before they could complete their scheme, the partners were compelled to file their schedule; as a consequence an official assignee was appointed to the estate, and the recent transactions of the firm came under notice. Evidence soon came to light of swindling, and the partners were arrested, as was also the master of the late *Snowbird,* and they were all charged with conspiracy to defraud. Enquiry as to the disposal of the goods the firm had purchased just prior to stopping payment, revealed the fact as to the fictitious nature of the *Snowbird's* cargo, and also of the despatch to Melbourne of a portion of the purchase for sale there. These goods were in charge of two men named O'Brien and Rogers. Immediately this fact became known to the assignee a warrant was obtained for their arrest, and telegrams sent to the police in Melbourne asking that the men should be apprehended. The telegram also stated that the goods had been sent by a certain steamer.

The officer in charge of the detective branch directed

Detective Christie to take up the case. His first object was to find out what had become of the goods, and on ascertaining that duty had been paid on them, and that they had passed through the Customs, he sought out the carter who had conveyed them away and from him learnt they had been taken to a well-known auction room in Collins Street for sale. He then called on the auctioneer, who informed him that the two men who were the ostensible owners of the goods had instructed him to sell them. They had asked him for an advance of £1,000 on account of the goods, which he readily gave by means of an open cheque. The men had arranged to call again the next day, but he had not seen or heard anything of them since, and, according to instructions, had sold the goods, which had fetched nearly £3,000. It was evident that they had received warning from Sydney that a warrant had been taken out there for their apprehension, and had felt that their only chance of avoiding arrest was to keep in concealment and be content with the advance they had received from the auctioneer.

Christie then called at the bank upon which the auctioneer had given the men the cheque, where the teller told him that he had cashed the cheque in question and had paid the men twenty £50 notes, all new. He also furnished a detailed description of the appearance of each man, for he had taken particular notice of them. The detective then went the round of the banks in Melbourne asking the officials of each to assist him in tracing the fugitives by informing him if the men or either of them in the course of the next few days should pay in or obtain cash or draft for any of the notes.

Next morning Christie received a message from one of

the banks to call, and, on calling, was informed that one of the notes had been paid in by the landlord of one of the hotels of Melbourne. Christie immediately proceeded to this hotel, and learnt from the landlord that he had taken the note and given change for it from a man who had a bundle of them in his pocket. The man had a friend with him and said they had come from Sydney. The landlord had not seen either of the men since, and did not know where they were living or anything more about them. He remembered, however, that a waiter had called a cab for them when they were leaving. This waiter was called and said he remembered the men quite well, and knew the cabman who had taken them away. He was then dispatched to find the cabman, and soon brought him to the hotel. Christie then engaged the cab, and, after picking up Detective Mainwaring at the City watch-house, the driver was asked if he remembered taking away two gentlemen from the hotel mentioned, and whether he could drive the detectives to the house to which he had taken them. This the cabman said he could do, and when they had arrived at the corner of Gertrude Street the cabman pointed out a two-storied house, which he said was the place where the two men had left him. As it was desirable before proceeding to the house to ascertain who the tenant was, and what character he (or she) had, Christie stopped at a chemist's close by and made enquiries from him. He was told the occupant was a widow, who kept a lodging-house and was a respectable person.

Whilst at the chemist's the detective wrote a memorandum purporting to be a request to a firm of solicitors that they would send someone at once to see the writer, and that the cabman who was the bearer of the memo. would point out the house they were desired to call at. The detective, leaving the cab a few doors away, knocked at the door of the house. The door was opened by a woman, who was evidently the landlady, and one of the detectives, assuming a strong Irish brogue, stated they had called to see Mr. O'Brien and Mr. Rodgers, and enquired if they were in.

"No," said she, "they do not live here."

"That is strange," said the officer, "because they sent this letter to our firm. They said they wished particularly to see us to-day on very important business."

The woman hesitated. At last she said, "Excuse me for a moment, while I go upstairs."

He replied, "Oh, as they are not here, we must hurry back to our office."

On hearing this the woman said, "Well, Mr. O'Brien and Mr. Rodgers are staying here, but they told me to say they did not. But as you are their solicitors I will tell them you are here. They are up in their bedroom."

The officers then remarked that they would go up with her. The woman made no objection, and they followed her closely up the stairs. She knocked at a door, which was opened by O'Brien, and Christie pushed into the room, saying, "We are detectives."

On hearing this the landlady opened fire upon them in most abusive terms. Taking no notice of her, however, they arrested both the men, searching their rooms and luggage, but without success. They were brought before the bench, but as no warrant had been received for their arrest, the police magistrate ordered their discharge.

## THE "SNOWBIRD" CASE.

The men left the court very jubilant, but the detectives, knowing the warrant would be over that day from Sydney, re-arrested them. The warrant duly came to hand. The prisoners were again brought before the magistrate and remanded to Sydney.

The detective was much puzzled as to what had become of the balance of the money which the men had received. He determined to again search the lodgings. It should have been related that when leaving the house with their prisoners, the landlady had invited Christie into her sitting room, where she apologised to him for the language she had used to him upstairs. She then produced a bottle of whiskey, saying, "I have got a drop of the real stuff here, and to show there is no animosity between us, you must have a nip." Christie affably complied.

With a view to propitiating the lady on his second visit, he brought a bottle of the best Irish whiskey. She conducted him into her parlour, where Christie produced his bottle, saying that as she had been kind enough to "shout" for him when he was last there, he had now brought some first-class whiskey to return her hospitality. The landlady was nothing loath, and the detective poured her out a regular "second mate's allowance," i.e., three fingers. After the lady had disposed of this he drew her on to talk about the recent arrest in her house. Then he pressed his fair friend to have just a trifle more, and desired her to keep the bottle to be finished at her leisure. The lady was much pleased at this, and expressed her appreciation of his generosity. Having thus loosened her tongue, Christie asked her permission to go upstairs and make another search in the men's room. To this she willingly assented. Calling the landlady after having finished his task, he examined her minutely as to the movements of her lodgers while they were in the house and especially asked her to tax her memory as to where they had been about the house or in the yard, or whether she could recollect having seen them in any other spot than their rooms or going up the stairs.

She said, "Now I remember that on the evening before they were arrested I heard someone on the landing upstairs and ran up to see who was there. Both men were there, and one of them was on his knees and part of the carpet was turned up. They seemed confused, and one of them said to me, 'You ought to have this carpet tacked down, as it is most dangerous. My friend's foot caught in it, and he slipped down and has hurt his knee.' I said I was very sorry and would tack it down immediately." The woman added, "But as it is a roll of notes you are after, if they were under the carpet, you would feel them easily enough." The detective then went to the spot where she had seen the men and ripped the carpet up, but no notes were to be seen. On examining the floor beneath, however, he observed a short loose board, which had evidently been cut to admit of the gas pipe in the hall below being got at. Prizing up this board and putting his arm into the cavity, he felt something soft, and found that it was a roll of new notes, the full balance of the money for the cheque.

His fair friend exclaimed, "Well, I never; you detectives are as cute as the devil!" Christie took the notes to the office, whence they were forwarded to the official assignee in Melbourne, who marked his appreciation of the detective's acuteness by sending him a present of fifty pounds.

As regards the swindlers, five in number altogether, they were duly tried and all convicted and sentenced to imprisonment. Four of them, including O'Brien and Rogers, received five years each and one two years.

This successful issue was due in a very large measure to the splendid work done by Detective Bowden in Sydney.

# PART II.

## AS ROYAL "SHADOW."

H.R.H. Prince Alfred, Duke of Edinburgh.
*(From a Photograph taken at the time of his Visit to Australia).*

Facing page 72]

Detective Christie as a Sailor on H.M.S. *Galatea*.
Disguise used while travelling with the
Duke of Edinburgh.

*Facing page 73*]

## CHAPTER IX.

### THE VISIT OF PRINCE ALFRED.

WHEN Prince Alfred, Duke of Edinburgh, second son of Queen Victoria, arrived at Adelaide in H.M.S. *Galatea,* on February 22nd, 1869, the Prince wrote to Captain Standish, then Chief Commissioner of Police of Victoria, enquiring if a brother to Captain James Christie of the 42nd Highlanders was serving in the Victorian Police Force, and asked, if such were the case, that he might be directed to wait upon him on board the *Galatea.* When Detective Christie presented himself in response to this command, it was arranged that he should be in close attendance on the Duke during his visit and exercise the greatest care that no undesirable characters approached the latter, and to take all necessary precautions to ensure his safety. This precaution was rendered necessary by the action of a fanatic who, in Sydney on his previous visit, shot at and wounded the Prince. Christie therefore in pursuance of his duty attended the Prince wherever he went night and day, accompanying him all over Victoria, and some amusing and interesting incidents in connection with the royal visit are to be related.

Some of the officers connected with the ship or in attendance on the Duke were young and full of high spirits. At this time the present Treasury Gardens had not been made, and at the back of the Treasury there existed a gully, which was subsequently filled in, and which led from the Treasury Buildings to the Fitzroy

Gardens. A few of these officers were much taken with the statue of Venus in the Fitzroy Gardens and, in a frolicsome mood, were carrying it to the Melbourne Club, where Captain Standish, Chief Commissioner of Police, resided, in order to put it into the Captain's bed. They had got it half way across the gully, when suddenly the moon shone out very brightly and disclosed the party to the eye of a vigilant constable. Seeing what looked like a party of men carrying a naked corpse, the constable ordered them to stop. The party took the alarm and promptly bolted in different directions, leaving the "corpse" on the ground. The constable gave chase, but in doing so fell head over heels into an unsavoury heap of refuse, and by the time he had recovered himself all trace of the men was lost. Next day Venus was restored to her pedestal, and nothing more was heard of the affair.

On one occasion the Duke informed Christie that a diamond ring, a gift from the Tzar of Russia, had been stolen from his room and desired him to endeavour to recover it. No trace could be found of the valuable article, but as a last resource Christie carefully overhauled the Prince's room, and the ring came to light hidden in one of the fingers of a glove the Prince had thrown aside.

The Prince, who resided at the Melbourne Club, went about the city a good deal incognito, and was always shadowed by Christie in his rambles.

Whilst the Duke was staying at the Club a rather funny thing happened. One of the members, a bit of a tuft-hunter, never lost the opportunity of making up to any member of the British aristocracy who might visit Melbourne. One day during the Prince's stay at the Club this member observed a tall fashionably-dressed man, apparently waiting for some one. The clubman immediately concluded that the stranger was a member of the Prince's suite. Accordingly he bustled round the club rooms to find some one who could introduce him. Not being successful in this, he determined to address the stranger himself, and approached him with some remark about the weather. The stranger was most affable, and replied in an English drawl that the country was much to his liking and the people everything that could be wished. The conversation was then proceeding, altogether to the satisfaction of the clubman, when Prince Alfred appeared. Seeing him coming, the stranger suddenly broke off, saying, "Pardon me, I must speak to the Prince." This confirmed the clubman in his supposition as to the rank and position of the gentleman he had been conversing with, and he determined to endeavour to foster the acquaintance so happily commenced.

That same afternoon the clubman called in at a tobacconist's in Collins Street to obtain a cigar, and whilst going in he was passed by a customer quietly going out, the same distinguished gentleman he had been talking to in the Club. He asked the tobacconist who that gentleman was who had just gone out. "Oh," the salesman said, "don't you know him? That is Detective Christie."

When the time came for his departure to Sydney, the Duke made Christie a present of a very handsome blue pearl pin mounted to represent a snake coil. The Prince expressed his great satisfaction at the manner in which

Christie had carried out his somewhat delicate duties. On the day of leaving, Christie accompanied the Royal party to Sandridge, where the visitors were to embark on the *Galatea*. Whilst standing on the pier, Prince Alfred came up to Christie and said to him that he was very desirous that he should accompany him during his entire trip in Australia and New Zealand. The latter said he was, of course, under orders, but that if the Commissioner approved, he would be very glad to go. A consultation then took place between the Governor (Sir Henry Manners-Sutton), the Premier, and Captain Standish, with the result that permission was given. As the *Galatea* was just on the point of sailing, Christie told Captain Standish that as there would be no time for him to return to the city to obtain his clothes, etc., he would have to go just as he was, and moreover that he had no money. Captain Standish then bustled round, and between himself and some of his friends got together the necessary funds and told Christie he should have his clothes sent after him. When Christie got on board he was very uneasy in his mind at being without his dress-suit and other clothes. The Prince's valet came to him and told him that the Duke had given instructions that he was to be fitted up with all that he required from the Duke's own wardrobe, including a brand-new dress-suit.

The duties devolving upon him in Sydney were much the same as what had been previously required,—attendance on the Prince at a constant round of balls, dinners, theatres, races, pigeon matches, etc. On the more private excursions the necessity for the protection of the

## THE VISIT OF PRINCE ALFRED. 77

Prince being recognised, Christie frequently assumed a disguise, often dressing as a sailor of the *Galatea*.

Whilst at the theatre one night, the gas being turned very low during one of the acts, Christie was standing at the back of the Royal Box and observed a dark object come whizzing down from the upper circle into the Royal Box, landing in the lap of the Countess of Belmore, the wife of the New South Wales Governor, who was sitting next to the Prince. In an instant (having visions of bombs, infernal machines, etc., in his mind) he slipped into the box, saying to the Countess, "Don't move," picked up the missle, ran out of the dress circle, and, without examining it, threw it down the back-stairs. On investigation it proved to be nothing more dangerous than a big bunch of flowers, which some enthusiast had thrown from the gallery to the Prince.

The *Galatea* reached New Zealand on the 11th April, 1869. Christie found a spot where the Prince might land in the evening, as he wished to go ashore incognito. It was beginning to blow very hard and the sea was getting up fast. The sailor Duke, however, insisted on leaving the ship punctually at 8 p.m. The boat was pitched about considerably. It then lifted on the sea, came down on the top of a pile, and stove in her bow. One of the men tried to stop the rush of water, which soon became knee deep. The boat was now in the breakers and being regularly pooped by the waves. The water was up to the thwarts, and it looked as if they would all have to swim for it. The Duke at this juncture took charge, issuing his orders as coolly and gamely as if on a river. Just as the boat was sinking, she grounded heavily. The crew patched her up in some way, mainly by stuffing clothes into the leaks, and managed to get her back to the *Galatea,* the sea having suddenly gone down as it frequently does in that harbour. Not to be beaten, the party changed clothes and started for the shore in another boat, and the Duke landed safely at the spot selected.

Next day the official landing took place. There was the usual round of festivities, in which the Maories took a great share, exhibiting native dances, etc. Fine sport was given to the Prince amongst the wild pigs, and during a chase of one the Prince fell into a ditch full of water but shot the animal and, although dripping wet, went to the assistance of a mounted policeman who was being attacked by a wild boar. The constable, however, killed the animal with his sword just as the Duke reached him.

Several robberies of jewellery at some of the leading hotels took place, and the local police were puzzled as to the culprit. The officer in charge of the police asked Christie to give him his assistance in discovering the thief. He immediately endeavoured, as usual, to obtain a "clue." His suspicions were directed to a man, a photographer, who, by representing to the Commodore who left Sydney for Wellington after the *Galatea* had sailed, that he was the Duke's own photographer and had missed his passage in the *Galatea,* obtained the Commodore's permission to have a passage in his ship to New Zealand. This man was staying at one of the best hotels and living in considerable style. There was little time to lose, so Christie determined to risk it and attempt a *coup de main*. He accordingly went to the hotel where the suspect was living and, going to his room, interviewed the photographer.

## THE VISIT OF PRINCE ALFRED. 79

"Oh, I beg your pardon," said Christie. "I see I have made a mistake in the room. I wanted to see a friend of mine about those robberies."

"What robberies?" said the man.

"Haven't you heard about them?" said Christie. "Why, the detectives have got on the track of the thief, and are now busy searching the room upstairs for him and his plunder. They are coming to this floor next, and I want to get my keys from my friend, with whom I left them, so as to be ready to show the detectives the contents of my portmanteaux."

The photographer turned pale at this, and without a word slammed the door on Christie's face and locked it. The window of this room opened on a balcony, and it was anticipated that if the occupant of the room was really the thief he would try and get off through this window, which was being watched from the yard by police. When the door was locked, Christie did not retire, but remained listening at it and distinctly heard the hurried opening of portmanteaux. He then knocked and called out in a feigned voice: "Open this door; we are detectives and must enter." With that the window was heard to be cautiously lifted. Christie had taken the precaution of opening the window of the room adjoining, which also looked on to the balcony, and, hearing the opening of the window, slipped into it and out on to the balcony, meeting the man as he stepped on to it. The police below were signalled to come up, and meanwhile the man was bundled back into his room. They found the whole of the stolen property on him, and he was duly tried and convicted of theft.

At the next port of call, the Prince at dusk, accom-

panied by Christie, who was dressed as a sailor, went
ashore incognito. The people were wildly enthusiastic
at the arrival of the Prince and the sight of one of the
crew of the *Galatea,* the first to be seen on shore, caused
them to give the latter the warmest of receptions, especially when he informed enquirers that he was the
Duke's coxswain. The Prince himself was not recognised, as he completely effaced himself, leaving Christie
to be the spokesman. The Duke was dressed in a blue
suit, wide-awake hat, and a big muffler round his neck.
No one recognised him, and he was much amused,
especially at the many and extraordinary questions which
were put to his "coxswain" as to the Prince's habits.
When they reached the gig and the officer in charge
saluted with the usual ceremony of receiving him, the
considerable number of people who had followed the
two down to the wharf saw who their visitor really was,
and raised a tremendous cheer as the boat shoved off.

On the next passage the corvette H.M.S. *Blanche* was
seen approaching on the weather bow with every stitch
of canvas she could possibly crowd on. Directly the
Duke noticed her he gave orders to pile on all the sail
the *Galatea* could stand, including upper and lower stun-
sails. The breeze was very fresh, and it was a pretty
sight to see both vessels bowling along, each under a
perfect cloud of white sheets. In spite of the *Galatea*
being the best sailer as a rule, on this occasion the
*Blanche* held her own, being of lesser draught and able
to keep nearer in shore.

At Canterbury the same festivities took place as at
other towns. It was at first intended that the Duke
should have been driven to Hokatika, to enable him to see
the magnificent scenery on the way out.

Information had been conveyed to the authorities that a party of Fenians had conspired to lay an ambush in the Otira Gorge and capture the Prince, take him into the mountains, and hold him as a hostage with a view to the settlement of the Irish question. The leader of the enterprise speaks of the matter openly to this day. The trip was therefore abandoned.

Amongst other amusements the Duke attended the races in company with Lord Charles Beresford, the well-known admiral and hero of Alexandria, and was very successful in backing horses. He then went to another town in the *Blanche,* the *Galatea* drawing too much water, and whilst there was driven further in a carriage with eight magnificent grey horses, the ribbons being handled by "Cabbage Tree Ned" (Devine), a celebrated coach-driver. Whilst at this place there was introduced to him a splendid specimen of a Highlander, who was a brother of the well-known John Brown, the personal attendant of the late Queen Victoria. The Duke attended the races, where he won £200 on "Captain Scot," a horse of Ned Devine's. When going to the races the Prince usually drove his own team of four horses, as he was a first-class whip.

During this visit a somewhat regrettable incident happened. A young lady made a wager with her *fiance* of a half-dozen pairs of gloves that she would at one of the celebrations walk up to the Prince and pinch his arm. The young man sent an anonymous letter to the Chief of Police, telling him what the girl meant to do. This letter was handed to Christie to take such action as might be thought necessary. He invoked the aid of the detectives, and they kept a watch on the young lady.

## DETECTIVE CHRISTIE.

On the day of the ceremony Christie kept on the *qui vive*, and, just when the Duke was talking to the Mayor prior to the opening ceremony, saw a detective standing close by a young lady in the crowd. This officer gave him a signal. At this moment the girl stepped boldly forward out of the crowd and started in the direction of the Duke. Christie at once intercepted her, and, raising his hat and touching her arm, said: "Good morning, Miss. I am so pleased to see you," addressing her as if she were a friend.

She was much taken aback, and said: "You are a stranger to me; please let me pass." As her way was blocked by Christie and, finding he did not move, she added: "I merely wish to just touch the Duke, and, if I do, will win six pairs of gloves."

Christie then informed her he was a detective and could not allow her to proceed as she wished, but the Duke would be glad to receive her in the proper form. She very willingly accepted the alternative, duly made her appearance, was introduced to and shaken hands with by the Duke, and, on leaving, received a box of gloves from Christie on the Duke's behalf.

The Duke had attended an exhibition of boxing by the local champion boxer and other pugilists, and, whilst Christie was chatting with his friends the next evening, a great discussion arose as to the real merits of the pugilists. As Christie was known to be an expert boxer, he was asked his opinion, when he replied that he thought the best way to settle the question would be for him to have a match with the champion himself. Directly this suggestion was made it was at once adopted, and a match was speedily arranged. The fight was with

Detective Christie and the Commissioner
of Police, N.Z.

On tour with T.R.H. the Duke and Duchess of York.

J. M. Christie and "Cabbage Tree Ned" (Devine).

*(Photographed in later years).*

*Facing page 83]*

## THE VISIT OF PRINCE ALFRED. 83

small gloves in a sixteen foot ring under the prize rules. After seven severe rounds Christie was declared the victor.

On the evening of arrival at the next port of call, the Duke wished to go ashore to the theatre incognito before his official landing, as he was not supposed to land till next day. Miss Cleveland was here playing in "Leah the Forsaken," and the Duke had a high opinion of her as an actress. Christie secured a private box at the theatre and inspected the streets by which the back entrance to the building could be reached, and found them a regular labyrinth. So, unobserved, he placed white chalk marks at each turn, so as to see his way after dark. The party landed about half-past seven, and by the help of the chalk marks found their way without difficulty. The Duke got back to the *Galatea* without being recognised.

At the conclusion of the visit to New Zealand, the Prince was proceeding to India, and not only wished to take Christie with him, but also to accompany him on his return to England to be attached to the Detective Branch of the Royal Household. Christie was unwilling to leave Australia, and accordingly returned to Melbourne, where he duly reported for duty on arrival. He had in his baggage some very handsome presents both from the Prince and members of his suite, the Prince's gifts including a gold watch and chain.

On the day of his arrival, Christie rigged himself out in fashionable style, frock coat, silk hat, patent leather boots, white spats and a gold-headed cane, and by way of a joke called in at the Detective Office, going into the room used by the public and knocking loudly on the counter with his cane. The chief clerk came out, and Christie, putting on the English Johnny drawl, said: "I want you to send a couple of detectives down to my hotel, where there has been a robbery." Mr. Robert Moore, the chief clerk, who recognised him at once, looked him up and down and replied drily: "By Jove, I think there certainly has been a robbery or a fire, and you have been in it." Next day the detective resumed his usual work.

* * * *

One day in April, 1901, the Governor-General of the Commonwealth, the Earl of Hopetoun, afterwards the Marquis of Linlithgow, sent for Detective-Inspector Christie and expressed his desire that he should hold himself in readiness to personally attend upon their Royal Highnesses the Duke and Duchess of Cornwall and York, now their Majesties the King and Queen, throughout their Australasian tour. It was generally understood that this step was taken upon a suggestion from the Imperial authorities in appreciation of Christie's services when in attendance upon H.R.H. the Duke of Edinburgh.

Needless to say the Royal "shadow" needed no tuition for his responsible task. Indeed, it might fairly be claimed that he was able to coach the Royal party's personal staff upon many points in relation to Australian popular customs and public characters. Of course, the staff in itself formed an efficient personal bodyguard, but they could not attend to the infinite details of purely detective duty. This is where Christie shone. He organised a plan of supervision which safeguarded the

## THE VISIT OF PRINCE ALFRED. 85

Royal visitors completely and unostentatiously. Nobody knew what was being done to watch and warn all suspicious persons, and to prevent intrusion upon the places reserved for the distinguished personages. Yet the services of the police and detectives, directed by their chiefs, in every State were called into requisition. Resorts that anarchists might frequent were closely watched. Knowledge had been sent in advance of a flight of confidence-men and pickpockets from Great Britain and the Continent, who were coming to Australia on predatory missions. These were all placed under surveillance by the various Police Commissioners in the different States. Christie alone, tall, straight, silver-haired, was in evidence, and few knew who and what he was. As one paper said he might have been an Ambassador or a Field Marshal in *mufti*.

Autographed Photograph and Gold Medal presented to Detective-Inspector Christie in 1901 by T.R.H. the Duke and Duchess of York on the termination of their Australasian Tour.

*Facing page 86*]

# PART III.

## AS CHAMPION ATHLETE.

## CHAPTER X.
## SOME PUGILISTIC ENCOUNTERS.

AFTER leaving the detective police force, Christie who had been victor in several contests with the gloves, was induced to further practise the art, and to engage in many encounters with well-known professors of pugilism. This is not the place to enter into a discussion as to the merits of pugilism, but it may be observed that at the time we speak of many men who occupied leading positions in the community were supporters of the art.

Christie, during his career in the ring, obtained a considerable Australian celebrity, and for a time was champion of Victoria. It would be tedious to recapitulate at length the various fights he was engaged in, but a few of the more important ones will be briefly narrated. Christie opened an Athletic Hall, in which he taught boxing, and he had considerable success as a teacher. In connection with the punching bag, which formed part of its appliances, a little incident happened which is perhaps worth relating. He had decided to fill the bag with wool, which was usually used for the purpose; and one of his pupils, a wool merchant, offered to give him what wool he required. The quantity required was comparatively small, and Christie was much astonished at receiving one day a whole bale of wool. This was placed on a small piece of vacant ground situated between the hall and the City watch-house. Enough having been used, the remainder of the bale was left near this door. There was at that time well known to the police a notorious thief, whose speciality was the larceny of wool and hides. One day he came into the hall and entered into conversation with Christie on the subject of his last conviction and lagging, and the thief was asked by the ex-detective why he was always stealing wool; Mr. Chirnside of the Werribee being desirous of learning what the man's *modus operandi* was and the reason for his penchant for the article. When looking round, this man noticed the bale at the door, and asked whose it was. By way of a joke Christie told him that it was stolen property, and that the watch-house keeper had placed it there pending the trial of the thief. "Look here, Mr. Christie," said the old lag, "now that you are out of the D.'s I know you will not give me away, so I do not mind telling you that if the wool is left there I intend to 'pinch' it. I know of a good fence with whom I usually do business, and he will stand for it."

Christie laughed at this, thinking the man was not in earnest; but that same night, somewhat late, when locking the side door mentioned, he was astonished at finding the old lag with a mate just hoisting the bale on to a truck. The pair were much taken aback at Christie's appearance, and the mate ran away, but was called by the ex-convict, who said: "Come back, you fool. Mr. Christie would not give us away." Christie then gave them warning that he would most certainly do so if they tried it on again, but the men were apparently not much impressed by what he said, and did not think him in earnest, for a few nights afterwards the wool had disappeared, and nothing more was ever heard of it.

## SOME PUGILISTIC ENCOUNTERS. 91

In October, 1875, Christie fought Abe Hicken, at that time Champion of Australia, for the championship and gold cup at the Princess Theatre. The fight was with 3oz. gloves, and lasted an hour and twenty-three minutes. It was held under ring rules in a sixteen-foot ring. Joe Thompson, the well-known "bookie," was referee, and, though Hicken was removed from the ring with two ribs broken, declared the fight to be a draw, though in Christie's favour. Subsequently, however, the reason for this singular decision became apparent, when it leaked out that the referee and his clique had been backing Hicken.

The following description of this fight is quoted in full from a characteristically-worded press report:—

The great glove fight, under Prize Ring Rules, for the Boxing Championship of Australia and a trophy valued £100 between Abe Hicken, the Champion of Australia, and Mr. J. M. Christie, Amateur Champion Boxer and Sculler of Victoria, took place at the Princess Theatre, Melbourne, on the 17th October, 1876. The theatre was packed to suffocation, and the whole of the proceeds were handed over to the sufferers by the recent disastrous wreck of the S.S. *Dandenong,* the prices for admission being £1, 10/-, and 5/-. Captain Aubrey, Superintendent of the Sailors' Home, acted as Treasurer.

Joe Thompson, the well-known bookmaker, much to the disgust of Christie and his friends, was appointed referee.

The combatants agreed not to claim any fouls so far as throwing was concerned.

At 8.30 p.m. they entered the ring accompanied by their respective seconds, Jack Thompson and Ned

Bitton for Hicken; Tom Curran, ex-Champion of Victoria, and Jack Cody for Christie.

Joe Thompson then advanced to the footlights amidst a storm of cheers and groans, and announced the weights of the fighters—Hicken, 10st. 9lbs.; Christie, 11st. 4lbs. After an appeal to the audience to keep order, he called time.

As the men advanced to the scratch and shook hands, their condition was the theme of general admiration. Hicken looked the beau ideal of a pugilist. His condition was all that could be desired. Christie looked the model athlete, his muscular development showing to great advantage as he threw himself into attitude.

Two finer or more accomplished boxers never entered a ring.

The preliminaries having been settled, both men shook hands and squared. The fun then began. By this time the theatre was crammed to suffocation.

1. Hicken faced his opponent in a playful style, while Christie looked determined and cool, but pleasant and gentlemanly. Little time was lost in sparring. Hicken began the work, evidently determined to let no grass grow under his feet. He let out and touched Christie's smeller slightly, Christie parrying the blow; a second effort reached his opponent's bread-basket, and he also landed one on the frontispiece. Each then let off both mauleys, and smart work followed. A rally ensued, both going down, Hicken under.

2. Hicken again showed eagerness, and reached Christie's dial-plate with his left, and escaped the compliment. It was now evident that Hicken was resolved to force the fighting, and it was whispered this was because

## SOME PUGILISTIC ENCOUNTERS. 93

his backers had bets that he would finish Christie off in the given time. Christie was evidently aware of the intention and at once assumed the easier role of defence. He met Hicken in the forcing and fighting, and returned a heavy impression on the ribs by a present on the jaw. Christie met him very coolly. After a magnificent exhibition of skill in attitude and defence both closed and were parted amidst a great round of cheers.

3. Short, sharp, and decisive, Hicken having the advantage. He went in like a demon, slogging on both sides.

4. During this round the seconds entered the ring, at the suggestion of the police, who were at the back, in order to prevent accidents when the men became excited. Christie met Hicken in first-rate style. He achieved marvels with his left hand, which went out like the piston of an engine, administering severe punishment. They were separated very early.

5. Christie still in fine form, striking Hicken's dial twice. Hicken lost his temper, and rushed in looking like a demon, but he was well met. Rally. Separated. The close was exciting, and cheer after cheer rent the theatre.

6. Hicken still forcing the fighting, but he was repulsed successfully. He got his head in chancery.

7. Hicken furious. He evidently thought he could knock Christie out of time. His backers were enthusiastic. Well met. Very short.

8. Abe began wild. Missed his right, but managed to land the left. Fine rally.

9. Very short. Hicken in chancery. Christie was perfectly cool, and retired to his corner smiling.

10. Hicken got at Christie's smeller. Repeated without return; caught Christie on the potato trap, but received a return in the same shot. Both went down.

11. Each succeeded in getting on the other side of the other's nut. Both seemed to be in a fair temper. Christie had the best of the round.

12. A desperate round. Hicken was again in tantrums, but found he had no (c)hicken to deal with. Christie got at his potato trap to more purpose, twice with those terrible left-handers of his. The audience began now to cheer Christie lustily. They had begun to notice that he was, as it were, alone—that the platform were almost to a man Hickenites. Hicken was also noticed to be doing all he could to annoy Christie. Christie's bark was peeled, and Hicken's kissers were puffed. His wind also seemed to be failing.

13. A fine round, Christie's hits telling with great effect, being delivered with marked precision and sledge-hammer force. Christie warded off several hits successfully, and was cheered to the echo.

14. Hicken evidently losing his first wind, and his condition telling. He was still forcing the fighting, and appeared anxious to please his patrons. Christie worked his dukes splendidly. He got a splendid hit at Hicken, but the latter slipped and fell. Groans and confusion.

15. Hicken came to the scratch in a terrible temper, and began to hit out wildly, but was knocked under the ropes.

16. Wind was evidently wanted on both sides, particularly on Hicken's. Abe got the best of this round, and got in repeatedly.

17. An undecisive round, Hicken getting very close,

## SOME PUGILISTIC ENCOUNTERS.

and showering blows, which were well warded off.

18. It now became evident that the surmises at the beginning were correct, and that Hicken was backed to win against time, hence his forcing of the fighting, a procedure that told greatly against himself. After a sharp rally Hicken got Christie under.

19. A fair round.

20. Christie nearly knocked Hicken over, but the latter recovered and a desperate rally ensued, the sparring being fine.

21. Good open fighting, with several exchanges, Hicken appearing to rally a little. The round closed in his favour.

22. A fair round, Hicken, after a desperate encounter, coming out best.

23. Hicken got in a straight blow and drew the claret. It may be noted that Hicken, in a most improper manner, used to draw his glove down Christe's face after "off" was called, as if to chafe the skin and annoy him. He also patted Christie on the head. Both men, however, appeared in good temper, one saying, "Isn't it beautiful?" to which the other replied, "Yes."

24. Having tapped the claret, Hicken made straight for Christie's rather prominent conk repeatedly. He was now getting his second wind, and had much improved his form in the 15th and 16th rounds.

25. Splendid hitting. Hicken seemed to be tired, while Christie's face was very raw. Christie got home repeatedly on Hicken's auricular apparatus.

26. Hicken appeared distressed. After a sharp rally they closed and separated as if done up.

27. More time was occupied over this round, as if the

opponents were resting. Christie stopped remarkably well, and in an unguarded moment caught Hicken below the gob very cleverly. Abe staggered back and was at once picked up by the redoubtable Jack Thompson.

28. Hicken's backers looked very blue. They had bet that he would polish Christie off in an hour, and now it seemed as if the fight would last all night. Christie got Hicken in chancery.

29. A bad round for Christie. Hicken got past his guards, and delivered three telling hits on his smeller. Great excitement. Many declared that Christie's legs were getting shaky.

30. Christie looked very raw and punished. He belied those who said his legs were giving by bearing himself firmly. Not once had he lost his self-control or temper. Nothing was done in this round.

31. Jack Thompson interposed when Hicken was severely gruelled, and evoked a unanimous howl of indignation. All the public were now in favour of Christie.

34. Both men were at it hammer and tongs, amidst immense excitement. So quick were the exchanges that it was difficult to note them. The men fought most determinedly, and seemed bent on giving the *coup de grace* to each other. The audience were becoming very demonstrative. One person in the stall seemed determined to interfere. The police authorities, afraid of a general *melee,* conferred with the referee, who jumped into the ring and closed the fight, which was declared a draw. Both contestants then shook hands, and left the ring in good humour.

Our illustration represents the moment when Christie, having been advised by his seconds that he had stood

Christie.   Hicken.
Finish of the 31st Round.
The Fight between J. M. Christie and Abe Hicken,
Oct. 17, 1876.

the assaults of Hicken for the hour on which so many wagers were hung, went in and dealt the sledgehammer blows from the shoulder which completely lifted the veteran off his feet.

The sale of the tickets to see the encounter produced £350, which was handed over to the fund for the sufferers through the loss of the ss. *Dandenong*. Christie won considerably over the event, as bets had been freely laid that he would be knocked out under the hour, and he had backed himself. His friends also were equally fortunate. His pluck in the performance was so much appreciated that he was tendered a complimentary benefit in the same theatre, at which all the cracks of the ring performed, and as a result he was handed £210 by the Committee.

When Jem Mace, the celebrated pugilist, who at the time was Champion of the World, was making a tour of Australia, Christie was engaged by Mr. Wilson, circus proprietor, who was financing the trip, to accompany Mace and box nightly with him four rounds, and also to meet all comers who might present themselves at any of the exhibitions given. For this he received £75 per week, while Mace's retaining fee was £150 a week with all expenses paid.

A recent writer in the press mentions that when Christie was appearing with Jem Mace the boxers proved a "most tremendous draw. They were got up in faultless style—white flannel knee-breeches, patent leather boots, flesh-colored stockings, and armless singlets. O, I tell you, they did pull in the cash."

Whilst under this engagement, Christie engaged most of the local cracks, and immense crowds attended the various performances in Sydney, Melbourne, and Adelaide. While under this engagement a bet was laid that he could not knock out Harry Sallars, a negro who was a leading professional, under ten rounds. An encounter taking place, in the second round Sallars nearly broke his opponent's jaw with a terrific cross counter and knocked out one of his back teeth. Christie was carried to his corner, where he spat out the tooth, which Mace picked up and said he would keep as a memento of the fight. At the third round Sallars evidently thought he would be able to finish off his antagonist very quickly, but the latter was on the alert, and contented himself for a little with just sparring for time to pull himself together. Sallars rushed at him with both hands and nearly tumbled him again, but Christie, recovering himself by a great effort and timing his blow to a nicety, gave the black a lovely left hander with sledge-hammer force full on the end of his nose, knocking him clean off his feet. The next round Christie gave him no time to recover, and after a very severe round the negro was done and gave in. Mace acted as referee in the fight.

A couple of days after the contest the two opponents met accidentally, and Sallars, coming up to Christie, said: "Well, Massa Christie, dey tell me dat I hab 'bout broke your jaw."

"There is nothing wrong with my jaw," said Christie, slapping with considerable force the right cheek, which was the uninjured one, but still causing himself considerable pain.

However, Sallars, knowing it was the other jaw which had been damaged, said: "Just do dat on the oder side, Massa Christie, and see how you like him." But Christie did not respond to the invitation.

## CHAPTER XI.
### HEAVY-WEIGHT CHAMPIONSHIP.

ON 12th August, 1871, Abe Hicken offered a cup of the value of ten guineas for competition for the amateur heavyweight Championship of Victoria. The contest was to be open to all comers, and was to be conducted at Hicken's Athletic Hall, under the direction of Abe Hicken, at that time Champion of Australia.

Though several men entered their names as competitors only two made their appearance on the evening of the fight. These were Jack Thompson and J. M. Christie. The Hall was crowded, although tickets for admission were ten shillings each. When the men appeared stripped for the fray there was great excitement. Each of the competitors seemed in splendid condition. Christie stood 5 feet 10¾ inches in height, and Thompson at 6 foot 3 inches. The former's weight was eleven stone and seven pounds, the latter thirteen stone and four pounds. Mr. Bill Branch acted as referee. Four ounce gloves were used. Both men entered the ring, which was sixteen feet square, and the contest commenced punctually at the appointed hour. The difference in height and weight between the two was very noticeable, and it was evident that so far as appearance went that Christie would have to do all he knew to hold his own. The feints were quick, and each man showed great ability in dodging the blows. First blood was drawn by Christie with a blow with his left on his opponent's nose.

Thompson then dashed in a left and right, which were however neatly parried. Thompson then rushed Christie to the ropes, having his face well peppered by the latter, but Thompson got in a smashing blow with his right hand right under Christie's left ear, which sent him staggering to the ropes, and thus ended the first round. On coming to scratch in the second round both men showed marks of punishment, Thompson's nose bleeding freely. Christie at once dashed in, landing a telling left-hander on Thompson's nose, and he replied wildly. Some sharp infighting then took place, during which Thompson slipped and fell, which ended the round. At this stage the betting became two to one on Christie. At the third round Thompson led off with a right cross-counter, which he landed on Christie's face, but before he could recover himself Christie sent him to the ropes, and the round was finished. Betting then rose to three to one on Christie. On the fourth round Thompson rushed at Christie with a left and right, but both were neatly parried. Some fibbing then took place, when Thompson sent in a left hander which Christie avoided very cleverly and replied by a cross-counter with his right on Thompson's jaw.

Although dazed the latter rushed to close quarters, when some infighting ensued, but soon a blow from Christie with his left floored his antagonist, and ended the fight in his favour. Christie was declared the winner, and received a great ovation from the spectators, who were much pleased with the fight, and also applauded Thompson for having fought well. The odds were certainly in favour of Christie's opponent, who had the advantage in height, length of reach, and weight, but science triumphed, and Christie in this fight certainly showed himself the better man and a severe punisher.

The cup was then presented to him by the donor amidst great applause.

Just before the Melbourne Cup meeting of 1878 a glove contest had been arranged by a well-known sporting surgeon, to take place at his residence in the presence of about forty of the *elite*. The match was to be between Abe Hicken and Jack Thompson and was to take place in the evening after dinner.

On the day appointed Abe Hicken was unable to be present, so Christie was approached with the view to taking Hicken's place. He consented, and he and Thompson met at the Doctor's to box for a cheque of £25. The dining-room was cleared and chairs placed round the room, as had been done on previous occasions. Some of those present, who had witnessed the fight at Brighton between the same contestants, expressed surprise at the improvement in Christie's physique, he having, owing to illness, weighed only 10 stone 10 lbs. on that occasion, and now weighed 11 stone 11 lbs., which was 4 lbs. above his fighting weight. This was none to his disadvantage in a contest in a warm room against an opponent about 2 stone heavier and 4 inches taller.

The contest lasted for twenty minutes, during which time six rounds, fast and furious, were fought, Christie being declared the winner and receiving the cheque amid hearty congratulations from those present. A well-known Captain acted as referee.

In a previous glove fight with Jack Thompson, Christie was the winner. In the one about to be narrated with the same antagonist Christie's good luck had departed, and he was defeated. A match had been arranged for the championship and £400. After being in training for about a month and getting into splendid condition, Christie became ill, and was sick right up to the time of the contest, and of course training was out of the question for him. He had lost more than a stone in weight, and was nine pounds under his proper scale. He was relying much on the friend who represented him in the negotiations relating to the match, and, when medical certificates were given that he was not in a fit state to appear in the ring, expected this friend to arrange a postponement of the match. At a consultation with Thompson this friend said no postponement of the fight ought to take place, and that if Christie could or would not meet his opponent the stakes must be declared forfeit. Christie was accordingly informed he must either fight or forfeit. Moreover, he had to leave in a waggonette in the morning at two o'clock for the scene of action at Brighton. The rendezvous was at the barracks in the St. Kilda Road, but although Christie was on time they had to wait two hours in the bitter cold for the referee. They got away about four a.m., and after a cold drive of nine miles reached Black Rock, beyond Brighton, where the fight was brought off at 8 a.m. After a game struggle, lasting nine rounds, Thompson was declared the winner. Mr. James Wilson, senr., of St. Alban's, the well-known racehorse owner, was referee.

J. M. Christie, 1848.

J. M. Christie, Champion Sculler of Victoria, 1876-8.

*Facing page 102*]

## CHAPTER XII.

### CHAMPION SCULLER OF VICTORIA.

FROM childhood Christie was at home on the water, having lived in his earliest years upon the borders of a lake in Scotland. As previously stated, too, he had considerable aquatic experience in Gippsland. So it was not surprising that in the 'seventies he became a champion of the river. He first won the Championship of Victoria on 8th April, 1876, when he defeated Messrs. P. J. Carter (champion), and the brothers, James and John Cazaly. He maintained his position for the two following years, when he was defeated by Charles Messenger. Christie has always acknowledged that he met more than his match, and he practically abandoned rowing, not only for this reason, but because he had decided to return to the Public Service, and had no leisure to devote to the arduous training which championship form in sculling entails. Messenger was a worthy successor. He was a finished oarsman, both by hereditary fitness and expert training. He was the son of James Arthur Messenger, himself a noted English oarsman.

During the whole of his period of river success, Christie trained under the tutelage of the late Mr. James Edwards, a well-known boatbuilder in his day, and probably one of the best-skilled men in Australia engaged in the construction of light river craft. Added to the advantage of having such an excellent coach, Christie possessed a fine physique. His style was finished and striking. He reached well over his toes, with both arms straight. He caught the water cleanly with a powerful horizontal stroke and used his force at the time of immersion, making a clean feather and a smart recovery. He was veritably a picture as he sat in his outrigger, and sent it skimming swiftly upon the smoothly flowing water.

There necessarily is not much that is sensational in an aquatic career, nor is it of general interest to row over again the sculling contests of the past. But Christie had adventures on the river all the same. At the finish of one race, for instance, which he had won by half a length, his sliding seat slipped, and he was capsized. Mr. S. Edwards jumped from the umpire's steamer and helped him back to the boat. Miss Emilie Melville, the reigning star in light opera in her day—the latter 'eighties, lived on the banks of the Yarra, and prevailed upon Christie to give her lessons in rowing, and she proved a very proficient pupil.

A very much less agreeable experience, though an amusing one, befell him one day when training on the Lower Yarra. He was rowing, as was his custom, in the buff, and, when passing some Harbour Trust works then in progress, was violently struck between the shoulder blades by a stone hurled at him from the bank. An ugly gash was inflicted and it bled copiously. Christie immediately pulled in and called upon some navvies to stop the miscreant, who was getting away as fast as he could. When the fellow was caught and brought back, Christie at once recognised him as a well-known criminal named John Sharp, whom he had arrested in 1868 on a charge of burglary at the residence of the then Mayor of Melbourne, Mr. A. K. Smith. Christie, who had been helped ashore and supported by the foreman of the navvies, felt a bit weak, but nevertheless said, "Well, Sharp, if you had hit me on the head instead of the back you would have finished me. But if you'll stand up and face me for four rounds I will cry quits." Sharp agreed, and a number of navvies formed an impromptu ring. Sharp was deservedly well punished, and ample justice was done. Christie then invited the foreman and about a dozen navvies to the Admiral Hotel, which stood where the Federal Coffee Palace now is, to drink his health. This Christie afterwards ascertained they did right royally. Twenty-two of them rallied to the hotel, and had two rounds each at Christie's expense. But he declares that he never settled with anybody so cheerfully as he had done with Sharp, and subsequently with the landlord.

As the outcome of a challenge issued by Christie to "row any *bona-fide* amateur in Australia a two-mile sculling match in outriggers, for a trophy of the value of £100 and the Championship," a contest was arranged between Christie and James Cazaly, "two of the best, if not the very best rowers in the colony," as they were described by a leading journal. This took place on Saturday afternoon, December 18th, 1875, the value of the trophy being £50; the course was on the Lower Yarra from the Melbourne gas works to Humbug Reach, a distance of very nearly two miles.

The following description of the race appeared in *The Australasian*:—

It is not often that we see so important a sculling match arranged and brought to an issue within so short a period of time as that which took place on Saturday last between these scullers. Only a fortnight before were the usual formal preliminaries entered into. In certain quarters this haste was regarded as unseemly, and expressions the reversal of complimentary were freely indulged in. It is, however, to be hoped that those whose feelings were so grievously wounded at the course pursued by Mr. Christie are now satisfied, at all events, that the race was one of the finest contests which has ever taken place on these waters. That it should have been rowed in the most unprecedented time, and won by feet only ought to go a long way to refute the suspicion that lurked in the minds of the Regatta Committee, when that body gave vent to its feelings in the resolutions passed at its last meetings. Whether or not the winner of the match on Saturday is entitled to be termed the "Champion Sculler" is not a matter of much concern at present; whatever Mr. Christie claims he is, no doubt, prepared to defend.

Soon after the advertised time, the steamer *Warhawk,* which had been engaged to accompany the race, left the Queen's Wharf fully freighted. On arrival at the starting place some delay occurred in awaiting the approach of the *Argyle.* As soon as that steamer had passed, the competitors took to their boats and rowed to their respective stations, where they were not long detained, having been sent off to an excellent start by Mr. H. A. Williams, who officiated as starter. Christie on the north side seemed to glide away quickest, but after a dozen stokes or so had been pulled, Cazaly showed slightly in front and soon assumed a lead of close on a boat's length; this he maintained for about a mile, when Christie drew up level, but Cazaly again assumed the lead, which he held down the last straight reach, but it was evident during the latter part of the journey that the leading man was closely pressed.

Cazaly began to row in the most determined manner, but his opponent could not be shaken off, and notwithstanding that the latter was allowed to get too close to the bank, which he struck with his scull on one or two occasions, he still held his own, and it became evident every stroke that a desperate finish was about to take place. On rounding the last turn—that is, that part of the river known as the commencement of "Humbug" reach—Cazaly steered too close to the Sandridge bank, while Christie hugged the opposite side. Cazaly's course proved too circuitous, for he lost his lead, and the wash of some four-oars in front completely extinguished his chance of making up his lost ground. Christie had in the meantime assumed a lead of half a length, which he managed to retain past the winning post, and won one of the best, if not the very best contested sculling races we have even seen rowed on our waters.

The winner used a sliding seat, which well nigh brought him to grief at the most critical part of the race. When at a short distance from the finish, Christie made a desperate effort, in response to a friend on the bank, for the lead. From some cause or other, probably the fouling of the sliding gear, or the great strength put into the last struggle, the seat went too far back, jumped up on the triangle piece, and stuck there hard and fast. There was, therefore, nothing for it but to struggle, which the winner did in a most determined and plucky style. This performance of Mr. Christie ranks him as about the fastest sculler we have yet had, the two miles having been traversed in about 10 minutes 12 seconds.

In consequence of Christie getting his left-hand scull entangled in strong rushes growing out from the bank, he was reluctantly treated to an immersion in the river. It was at first feared, when Sid Edwards was seen to jump into the river after the distressed sculler, that Christie had become exhausted, and had fallen in that condition from his boat. Such, however, was not the case, for though the severity of the race left its marks on him, there was still a trifle left. It is a pity that the course was not fixed so as to have a straight finish. Mr. Arthur Nicholls acted as umpire.

On April 8th of the following year, Christie won the Challenge Sculls (Australian Cup) at the Melbourne Regatta. The competitors were Christie, John and James Cazaly, and P. J. Carter, and the greatest possible interest was taken in the race, as the title of Amateur Champion Sculler of Victoria went to the victor. As a newspaper report says:—"Christie was favourite from his late performances, and the fact that he had paid every attention to his training. When the race started he soon singled himself out in the front, and before half the race was over was at least a hundred yards ahead. Carter found himself in hopeless difficulty early, and therefore did not persevere. In the last half of the race, Christie allowed John Cazaly to come nearer to him on sufferance, but there was no sign of a race, owing to Christie's great superiority. Time, 9min. 17sec."

On March 20th of the following year Christie also won the Champion Sculls at the Barwon Regatta, Geelong, four days later easily winning the Champion Sculls and Australasian Cup from James Cazaly and W. Stout at the Melbourne Regatta. He then left for Sydney by the s.s. *Lyee-Moon* under engagement to Mr. John Wilson for boxing matches with the famous fighter, Jem Mace.

Christie was eventually beaten for the Sculling Championship of Victoria by Charlie Messenger, son of a former Champion of England.

Christie in his career was also a foot racer far above the average, and also was in great demand as a trainer of athletes, and so it may be truly said that he achieved prowess in the ring, on the river, and on the road.

After four years of athletics, Christie received an offer to return to the Government service, which he accepted, and eventually joined the Customs Department as Detective.

# PART IV.

## AS CUSTOMS DETECTIVE.

Detective-Inspector Christie with Officers and Police during the raids on the Illicit Distillers in the Warrnambool District.

[facing page 112]

Illicit Still Hunting

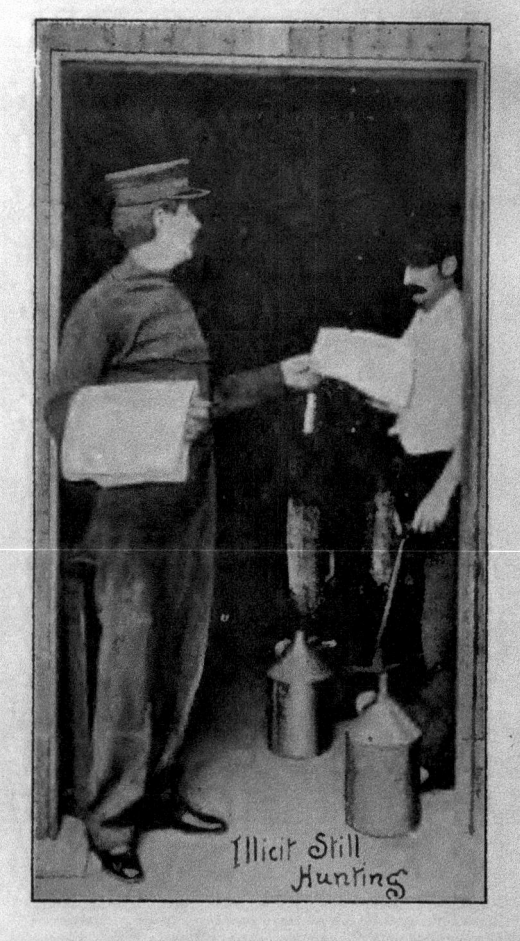

Detective Christie sells "The War Cry."

Facing page 113]

## CHAPTER XIII.
## ILLICIT DISTILLATION.

THE operations of the men engaged in the illicit manufacture of spirits were often conducted in a highly ingenious manner, and with great daring. The loss to the revenue was considerable. Public-housekeepers of a certain class were always ready customers of the "moonlighters," as they could purchase spirit for about 5/- per gallon and sell it across the bar in noblers at sixpence a piece; whereas, the duty-paid article would cost them say sixteen shillings per gallon at the least.

Another evil was the prevalence of drunkenness in the illicit still districts. The drinking bouts which often took place in the small townships or villages in the bush were frequently the cause of scenes of debauchery of the most shocking kind, and were a scandal to the community. But the greatest possible difficulty was experienced in detecting the site of the stills, and, what was more important, in obtaining evidence of such a conclusive nature as to cause the conviction of the person engaged in the illicit traffic. If the still were situated in a broken and mountainous district sparsely inhabited, the chances were that the surrounding inhabitants were more or less interested in the trade and all on the alert to give warning of the approach of the revenue officers or of any strangers coming into the district who might be suspected of being such. Moreover, the capture of a still itself was of comparatively little service, unless the persons who worked it were also caught. A few feet of pipe formed into a worm and a few vessels would be sufficient for the bare making of spirit, and could easily be replaced if taken.

Stills were located in all kinds of places and neighbourhoods. Sometimes they would be found in a lonely valley in the mountains, and approached only by secret paths through wild and thick forests. So well concealed were some of these stills that anyone in their neighbourhood could hear the workers actually talking to each other and yet be quite unable to locate the exact spot. From such places the spirit would be distributed to purchasers by means of packhorses. Even when settlers did not approve of the traffic they were unwilling to give any information, as the relatives and friends of the distillers would not hesitate to seek vengeance. Sometimes a still would be situated right in the city in one of the busy streets, either on business premises or in a private house. The stuff would be taken round in all kinds of innocent-looking conveyances, some of which will be described presently.

The most effective ways of obtaining information were found by the Department to be the employment of special agents, who would settle or work in the suspected neighbourhood, and also by the payment of large rewards, such as a hundred pounds in gold coin. This money would be paid without disclosing the informant's name and identity in any way, no official receipt being taken. The bait of such a reward was often too much for many. Sometimes also other motives than gain operated on the informers, such as spite, revenge, or jealousy. On one occasion, for example, the Head was interviewed by a

## ILLICIT DISTILLATION.

woman who said she desired to give information about a still, and it came out she was the wife of the man carrying on the trade. There was another woman in the case, and the man had left his wife without support. She was consequently justified from her point of view in making what she could out of him. The operations of these illicit distillers was a continual worry to the Department, which tried hard to suppress them.

In the Western District of Victoria there was at one time established a regular gang of smugglers, who, though nominally settlers or small "cockatoo" farmers, yet practised every kind of lawlessness, and were a terror to their more respectable neighbours, who were, however, few and far between. The first time the officers came into contact with this notorious gang was at the wreck of the ship *Fiji* at Moonlight Head, close to where the wreck of the *Loch Ard* took place. The shore was strewn with wreckage of all descriptions, including a large assortment of dutiable goods. A posse of Customs Officers, of whom Detective Christie was one, was therefore sent down to protect the revenue. They had not long arrived when they soon found that the gang was hard at work. On one occasion, whilst removing some packages, they were interrupted by a Customs Officer, but they immediately assaulted him, and he was thrown over a cliff at least four hundred feet high. He fell about fifty feet, but, fortunately for him, into a bush, which he caught and clung to till rescued. The members of the gang who committed the outrage were afterwards arrested and convicted.

The leader and moving spirit of the gang was an Irishman, known as Denis O'Brien, a thick-set man of great muscular power and daring conduct. This man was one of those convicted, and was removed to the local watch-house. Christie, knowing the man had had nothing to eat that day, had a meal supplied to him, and when passing the lock-up later was hailed through the barred windows by O'Brien. "I got that bit of breakfast you sent me in this morning," he said, "and I was very thankful because I was jolly hungry." To which Christie replied, "Oh, that is all right, Dennis; though I had to 'jug' you, I did not want to starve you also." The man then said he would send the officer a nice keg of poteen as a Christmas gift, real good stuff, that would make the detective's hair curl. To which Christie laughingly replied, "Thanks, my boy, and mind you do."

A little while after this, Christie was directed to see the Head of his Department in the latter's office. Dr. Wollaston told him that he desired that effective measures should at once be taken to put a stop to the operations of this notorious gang. The credit of the Department was involved, and they must bestir themselves and not rest till the gang was entirely suppressed. To this Christie replied that the task would not be an easy one, the men were a desperate lot, known to stick at nothing, and the attempt to capture them would involve considerable danger. Still, of course, he would willingly take the matter in hand. The Doctor then said, "Well, I shall give you a free hand in this matter, and will back you up in any action you may advise me is necessary, and you shall have as many men as assistants as you may require. I need hardly tell you, however," he added, "that absolute secrecy is required, and that you cannot be too

Detective Christie as a Travelling Tinker.

*Facing page 116*]

Detective Christie as a Travelling Tinker.

Reading Warrant to Tom Delaney at Warrnambool Watch-house *(see page 134)*.

*Facing page 117*]

cautious. Above all, see that none of our good friends in the press get any inkling of what is in the wind, or else we shall have some of those delightful paragraphs in the papers and such headlines as 'Customs on the Warpath,' 'Suppression of Moonlighters,' or 'Strenuous Action by the Permanent Head and His Officers," and so on, and the whole thing will be 'blown upon.' " Christie assured the Doctor he would employ only the most discreet of assistants.

After some consideration, he determined that the method most likely to lead to success was in the first place to obtain a thorough knowledge of the geography of the district, and of the various settlers dwelling in the suspected neighbourhood, and so endeavour to locate the actual sites of the stills. He decided, therefore, to adopt the guise of a travelling tinker. As, however, he know nothing about tinkering, he betook himself to an acquaintance who was a member of a well known firm of tinsmiths in the city (Lanyon and Bryant). His friend (Mr. Bryant) told him that with a little application, he could, in a few weeks, learn sufficient of the craft to pass doing merely rough jobs. Thanks to this friend's kind help, Christie learnt all that would be required. Having sent on his kit tools together with the suitable rig-out for a "swaggie" to a trusty friend in the district, Christie soon followed, and quietly turned himself into a travelling tinker. When starting on his rambles his friend warned him, "If you make a false step," he said, "or give yourself away in any particular, you will be bowled out at once. The gang would soon settle you, as they had often been heard to boast that if they ever caught any 'sanguinary' detectives near the scene of their operations, they would make poteen out of them, the same as the moonlighters did to the ganger Fitzpatrick in Ireland." Christie was well armed with weapons concealed, and said that two could play at the same game.

He set out in the direction of the locality where O'Brien lived, about twenty miles distant. Having gone about eight miles, he camped on the edge of a small lagoon known as the "red water hole," and whilst so doing, a mounted constable came along and questioned him as to his name, etc., and generally putting him through a severe cross-examination. The constable then told him he would have to search his swag because some larcenies had been committed in a neighbouring township, and that Christie answered the description of the suspected thief. The constable found nothing in the swag. Christie took off his coat and waistcoat offering them for examination also. This he did because he was afraid that the constable would detect the arms he had under his singlet. The constable then went on his way, without having the least suspicion who the tinker really was.

Christie travelled on for a few days, calling at all the houses on his way, and executing any repairs that might be required. One settler would send him on to another to see if he could get a job, and by using the names of these people, the person to whom he was sent, regarded him as a *bona fide* professional tinker travelling only in the search for work. At one of these places, he executed some small jobs, amongst which was that of repairing a boiler. For this he took a shilling and a meal in payment. This place was close to where the distillers' headquarters were supposed to be, and the detective doubled his precautions. At last, he came to the house of the leader O'Brien, and found his wife on the premises. The latter gave him a few jobs. He then went on his way, but had not gone far when she called to him and said, "If I thought I could trust you, I have a job which I want done badly." To this he said, "Of course, you can trust me; you may be sure I do not want to lose a job, and any way I am not the person to peach. If there is anything crooked in the wind, I am not so fond of those D's as to wish to do them a good turn, and why should I give you away? What is the job?" She replied, "I have a copper pipe which wants mending, but it will take you a good time to do, and will want a good deal of work. I am afraid that damned fellow Christie might come round, and catch you at it. If he did, he would twig what the article was at once, and we should all get into trouble." "Why do you think Christie is about?" said the tinker. "Oh," said she, "don't you know he was down the forest about a month ago and seized Long Will's still, and had him convicted?" "Oh, yes," said the pseudo tinker, "but I have no truck with coves of that breed. I know he would as soon jail me as anyone else if he nicked me making a still or worm for any of the boys, but I am too fly for him. I can do any job without him spotting me, smart as he may think himself, and I can do him with his eyes open. Those D's think a damned sight too much of themselves, and I like taking them down a peg when I get the chance." With this speech, the woman seemed satisfied that the tinker could be trusted, as she said, "Denis is away from home, but I will go and get the worm for you to see if you can mend it; it got broken by one of the horses getting loose and treading on it. It is kicked about so much it is quite useless." After telling him to sit in the kitchen to await her return, she left to fetch the worm.

There were two children left in the house, with whom Christie endeavoured to make friends, at the same time trying to observe the direction the woman had gone. Christie said to one of the girls, "I will put my billy on the fire, and make myself some tea, as your mother will be some time if she has far to go." The younger child immediately burst out, "Oh, she won't be long; she has only gone across the creek to Leach's to get the pipe." The sister turned on her savagely, telling her to shut up. However, the long-sought-for information had been obtained. In about a quarter of an hour Mrs. O'Brien returned, and told Christie he would find the worm on the other side of a stack, which she pointed out, adding, "Mind; that stack is not on our selection." She said this because in the case of discovery it would be important to show the worm was not on O'Brien's property.

Christie got the worm, and saw it was beyond any skill he possessed to make it good, and suggested to the lady that it would be much better to get a new worm. He said he could get her a splendid one made of copper and infinitely superior to the damaged leaden one for a sum of five pounds. "Oh," said she, "it is all damned easy to talk about getting a new one, but the —— Detectives are on the job, I suspect, and we could not manage to get it here without being caught." On this the tinker assured her she need have no fear on that point. He himself would undertake to convey the worm safely to her, and neither Christie nor any other of the sanguinary D's would detect it, as he would put it in a

## ILLICIT DISTILLATION.

bag of chaff, and bring it down by the back track himself, so that nobody would be any the wiser. "Well," she answered, "if you can undertake to get it here before Christmas I will take it," and was assured she should have it without fail, but the tinker said, "What about the money; will your man pay down on the nail?" "You need not be afraid," said the woman; "your sugar will be all right; you may take your oath of that."

Christie then returned to his friend's place, resumed his usual garb, and at once returned to Melbourne to make arrangements for making the raid. Arrangements were made with Mounted-Constable Arthur, at Cobden, for the assistance of the constables in the district, and a secret telegraph code was agreed on.

The party was to meet on the night previous to the day upon which the surprise was to be attempted. Detective Christie and a Customs Officer, well armed, proceeded by train to Camperdown. Christie took with him the make-up of a "sundowner," and his swag, including in his outfit a boot with an iron attachment which would have the effect of causing anyone using it to limp in walking. At Colac he changed his clothes, and soon transformed himself into a veritable "sundowner." On the platform at Camperdown he limped along, stooping to make himself appear several inches shorter. No one took much notice of him except some urchins, one of whom remarked, "That old man has a stringhalt." On the way out he bumped against one of the local constables, who said to him, "Can't you see? Where the devil are you going to?" Christie made no reply, but passed on down the road, where he met some other members of the party. They all went to the Police Station, and until explanations were made the sergeant in charge thought the disguised detective was a prisoner whom Mounted Constable Arthur had brought in. "Well," he said, "no one would recognise Christie in that disguise." He handed him a telegram, and told him in case he did not get out at Camperdown, he had sent a constable up to the railway station with a copy of it to give him. Christie told the sergeant that he had met the constable, and that, owing to his having one eye bandaged, did not observe him till he had cannoned against him. "We will have a little joke at his expense." Just as he had said this, the constable entered much out of breath, saying, "He has not come; I looked through the whole train, and Mick, the guard, assured me he was not on board, or else he would have seen him." "Oh," said the sergeant, "that will be all right; we shall get a wire from him in the morning. In the meanwhile, just look that old man up and enter a charge against him of insulting behaviour." The constable accordingly said, "Come along, old chap, and I will put you in the logs." On Christie raising his head and smiling, the constable exclaimed, "Why, this is the old chap who nearly knocked me over at the railway station." He was much disconcerted when the whole party then burst out laughing, but enjoyed the joke, saying, "Why, this is the second time that beggar has taken me down," referring to the search of Christie's swag when he was camping in the forest. Final arrangements were then made to meet on the following night.

The next day the officers kept under cover till dusk, when, according to appointment, a butcher's cart was driven into the yard of the Police Station. The officers lay down in the vehicle, and were covered up with corn sacks. They were then driven about eight miles out, where a constable joined them with horses. The party mounted and proceeded through swamps up to the saddle flaps, and over ranges till the red waterhole was reached. On arrival, Constable Arthur imitated the note of the mopoke, which was the agreed signal, and immediately had a response. All these precautions were very necessary, because if any of the settlers, "cockatoos," or wood splitters had noticed them, a bush telegram would have been sent through the forest immediately to warn the gang. The night was very dark, and the route lay over most difficult country, mountains, gullies and creeks; these obstacles making rapid progress impossible. After a toilsome and hazardous march the river was reached, at a spot where a bridge should have been, but it had been washed away. As the river was running a "banker," there was no help for it but to try to cross on another bridge about three miles higher up. Constable Arthur proposed to swim the river. The suggestion was not acted upon, as to attempt to swim across would seem only to be courting disaster. There was no alternative than to push on and attempt to reach the other bridge in time. The already jaded horses had then to be hurried on, but, considering the nature of the road they had to travel, it was not easy to hasten them much. The object was to reach the spot where the still was supposed to be located just before daylight. The bridge was at last reached, and, much to their relief, found to be still standing, although a foot of water was running over it. The timber of which it was built was very shaky, and the structure looked as if it might collapse at any moment. The spot on the river where it was situated was known as the "Devil's Punch Bowl," on account of the eddies of the river at that point. The party had to risk the passage, and by great good luck all crossed in safety. Hardly, however, had they done so when, with a roar and a crash, the bridge disappeared beneath the flood and was swept away down the stream.

Encouraged by their success the party traversed a precipitous gully, close to which lay the shanty of a notorious sympathizer of the gang, who was known to have a yelping dog always on the alert. It was tolerably certain that they would be discovered unless the dog could be disposed of or quieted. A lump of meat had been brought as a precaution, duly "doctored." One of the constables then dismounted and proceeded to interview the animal. The constable soon returned, announcing that the cur had been brought to terms, and they need not trouble more about him.

Quickening the pace, and after a fearfully rough journey, they eventually reached their destination a little before two, fortunately in good time but much fatigued by the journey. A fire was quickly lighted in a quiet and concealed spot, and a billy was boiled, which enabled them to have some hot tea (with a stick in it) and a snack of food. Whilst thus engaged they heard the sounds of a horseman coming up at a rapid pace over the track they had just traversed. As the man came close enough to be recognised, it was seen that he was the occupant of the farm they had passed, and that they had been much in error in supposing that they had got by his dwelling without notice. The man was riding rapidly past the party when he was hailed and desired to bail up. He, however, took no further notice than to urge on his horse faster. Christie then jumped on his horse and, with two constables, galloped after and bailed him up in the most approved style. Of course they had no legal right to do so, but, as they well knew what his errand was, it was clear if they had allowed him to pass no possible chance of a capture would remain. To put a good face on the matter, Christie addressed him as if he were a most worthy and respected citizen, and, putting on his most winning manner, said, "Mr. Murphy, I regret exceedingly the necessity for stopping you, but as I understand from Constable Arthur, whom you know, that you are a decent, law-abiding man, I must call upon you in the Queen's name, and by virtue of the authority which is vested by law in Her Majesty's Customs Officers, to demand your assistance in the affair in which we are engaged. I am Detective Christie, and the officers with me are constables." "I thought as much," replied the man; "but I'm damned if I help you one little bit." "Oh well," was the reply to that, "we do not care very much, but you will have to stay with us. You will get three months' 'hard' if you give us any trouble." Seeing he could not help himself, the man gave in.

The time had now come for action. Weapons were looked to and a start made for the house of the leader of the gang. Just before daybreak they sighted the shanty of the leader's brother, and in nearing the place Murphy became very uneasy, and was evidently much alarmed. He then burst out, "For the love of Heaven let me go back, boys; for if they see me with you they will think I have informed against them, and my life will not be safe."

On consideration as he could now do no harm, and as it was evident that all he desired was to be permitted to return home, they allowed him to go, warning him, however, that he must return directly to his shanty, and that they would keep an eye on the track to see that he did so. Murphy having sworn by all that he held most sacred that he would do as desired, immediately went off at a hard gallop down the track towards his home. Next O'Brien's house was visited.

No signs of a still or of distillation were found. A Customs assistant with a constable was despatched to search Wilson's house on a small selection close by, Christie following shortly after them. This was about 6 a.m. Wilson was found to be up and another man in bed on a sofa in the kitchen. On Christie's arrival a search of the buildings was made, and at a room in the back detached from the main building was found a complete still, with all the apparatus necessary for working it set in a fireplace, together with some spirits. Wilson admitted the building and still were his property, but declined to say from whom he had got the latter. The worm, however, was not found in the premises, and, on being questioned where it was, Wilson averred he did not know, saying that "they" usually brought it there at night and took it away when they had done. He refused to say who he meant by "they" or give any information as to who his associates were. On further questioning, he admitted he made the spirits which had been found. On making this admission both Wilson and the other man were placed under arrest.

There were three large vats in the room which the officers desired to remove with the still, and on Christie's

## ILLICIT DISTILLATION.

observing that it would be necessary to pull the building down to get them out, Wilson showed that the sides of the building were movable, and that by displacing them the vats could be taken out easily. The building was fitted up very completely as a distillery, the drain for the waste being concealed and ending amongst a lot of ferns adjoining the still house. A quantity of malt was found buried in the garden. Outside the fence was a well about four feet square containing water, which was up to within ten feet of the top. The sides of the well were boarded up, and the top was boarded over with a hole in the covering large enough to admit of a man. One of the constables called Christie's attention to a ladder which went down the well, and upon the latter going down he observed a round hole in one of the sides from which projected a brass tap. The constable then dug down the side of the well to see what was there, and at about a foot from the surface came on top of a quarter cask. The cask was lifted out, and the contents were found to be spirits. Wilson was asked who buried the cask in the spot and admitted he himself had done so, and also that the spirit had been made by himself. The evidence now being all complete, the prisoner was taken away and lodged in the lockup. He was subsequently brought before the Court and convicted.

It may be mentioned in connection with the capture of stills in the Western District, that months were spent by Detective-Inspector Christie in his attempts to discover the offenders. During that time he assumed various disguises, but on no occasion was his real character detected. The only persons in his confidence were a trusty friend who lived in the district and Constable Arthur. Through the help and assistance of these two, Christie, while camping out, was supplied with food, which was hidden in a zinc-lined case sunk in a hole in the ground. Anyone visiting his camp would see nothing but an old tinker living apparently on damper and scraps which he obtained from the people around. Two plans of the district were prepared, in which all bush tracks, gullies, streams, etc., were minutely set out, and new names given to these and the various localities. A cypher code was also arranged, in case any letter passing between Christie and his confederates got astray. These precautions were very necessary, because some of the youths employed in the local post-offices were related to the illicit distillers, and would perhaps "spot" any communications of a suspicious nature.

The stills in this district were so numerous and situated such distances apart that it was hopeless to attempt to capture them all simultaneously, and accordingly it was necessary to take only one or two at a time. When the capture of two or three had taken place it was the detective's habit, in order to disarm suspicion and lull the uncaught moonlighters into a false security, to "blow" considerably to the representatives of the local press and intimate that the practice had now been effectually stamped out and no more stills existed. Then the persons still carrying on the game would chuckle to themselves and think how the detectives were being fooled, but after a short period of quiescence the detectives would be again in the field and some more of the stills nabbed. The reporters used to get rather irate at being misled in this manner, and did not hesitate to

## ILLICIT DISTILLATION. 129

inform Christie that in their opinion Ananias was a pillar of truth as compared with himself.

At this time a short-lived Warrnambool paper desired to publish a likeness of Christie in connection with the report of a seizure, and, not being able to obtain one in time reprinted a portrait of the then Governor, Lord Hopetoun, who, at the time the picture was engraved, wore a small moustache, as did the detective—this being perhaps the only characteristic common to both. Lord Hopetoun was much amused at this incident, which is still well remembered by the Victorian press. A small reproduction of this portrait is here given.

DETECTIVE INSPECTOR CHRISTIE
The Earl of Hopetoun as Detective Christie.

## CHAPTER XIV.
## THE LAST OF THE "MOONLIGHTERS."

SOME weeks after the conviction of Edwards it became apparent that illicit distillation had not been put a stop to in that district. On the former occasion the worm of the still could not be found. Subsequently the services of black trackers were obtained, with a view, if possible, of finding what had been done with it. By their help the place where the worm had been secreted was found, but the worm had been removed. A thorough search was made for miles round, but nothing was discovered except certain tracks, which, however, incidentally gave the clue to the existence of another still. Under cover of darkness the police paid several visits to the suspected locality, and succeeded in tracing the worm to the vicinity of a small creek situated about three miles from the house of some suspected "moonlighters." This creek at the particular spot was in the heart of the forest, and the banks were partially obstructed by trees and thick undergrowth. The little stream was subsequently appropriately named "Whiskey" Creek. The locality was visited several times by Christie in company with Constable Arthur. Night after night the detectives pursued their search, often camping out and sleeping in hollow trees. After several of such visits they came to the conclusion that the still they were in search of must be somewhere within a certain radius and that the time had arrived to endeavour to catch the moonlighters in *flagrante delicto,* their apprehension being of more importance than the seizure of the mere still. Accordingly, at nine o'clock one night four men, well mounted and attired in orthodox bushman's style, met by appointment at the Boggy Creek bridge. The party consisted of Constables Arthur, Snowden and Jones, all first-class bushmen, and Detective Christie. Constable Arthur told his comrades that two men, being those suspected, and a dog had been seen going through the forest in a certain direction. Leaving the horses, the party proceeded on foot towards Whiskey Creek. Rain was falling, the darkness was intense, and not a sign apparent to indicate the way through the thick bush. Arthur, however, was their guide and kept them on the right track. Reaching a belt of almost impenetrable scrub, they halted to determine their next move, and, while conversing in an undertone, voices apparently proceeding from the centre of the scrub came to their ears.

"I can hear them," said Constable Jones, "and am sure that is Tom Delaney who is speaking."

It was now about two o'clock in the morning. A consultation was held in whispers and a plan of action decided upon which it was anticipated would enable them to completely surround the spot and obtain absolute evidence of the manufacture of the spirits and ensure the capture of the operators. With the utmost caution and the greatest difficulty they penetrated the scrub. The voices could still be heard, and the speakers were evidently not more than 150 feet distant, but the bush was so thick that not a gleam from their fire could be seen. The men were talking loudly, and the frequent splashing of water could be distinctly heard. Gradually, foot by foot, and as noiselessly as they could, the police forced their way through the tangle, and after a full hour's struggle at last obtained a clear view of the still house. A curious scene was opened up to them. Within a few feet of where they stood, in a small cleared space, stood a little building—a mere "gunyah" constructed of rough saplings. At one end was a chimney, in which a bright fire was burning under a large still, and on the top of a vat was a kerosene lamp, which completely lit up the shanty and enabled the officers not only to recognise and identify the men but to see everything they were doing.

The men were at the moment engaged in the manufacture of whiskey, and were talking cheerfully, quite unconscious of the presence of the officers who were watching their movements. The latter placed themselves as quietly as they could around the building, but in so doing one of them stepped on a rotten branch. Love heard this, and peered forth into the darkness, looking right at one of the party who was standing not sixteen feet away from him. However, owing to the darkness, and probably somewhat blinded by the glare of the lamp, he did not observe the watcher, but, speaking to Delaney, said: "Tom, I am sure there is someone about." Delaney said: "Oh, it was only a 'possum you heard. There is no one, you may be sure," and the two went on with what they were doing. Christie then, drawing his revolver, rushed into the shanty and, covering the men, called out: "Customs. I arrest you, Tom Delaney and Jim Love." At this time the detective thought the sides of the gunyah were of bark and that the men could not get through them before he reached them. The moonlighters looked up in dismay, whilst Christie advanced, pointing his weapon, saying: "Stand, or I'll fire; you are my prisoners." With that one of the men bolted away, ducking his head through the sacking, calling out to his mate, "Come on, Jim." The latter immediately followed, and the officer fired two shots, more with the object of alarming them than hitting them. The still stood in the way, and it was impossible to intercept them before they got through the side of the building. Constable Jones outside also fired, but without effect. The officers rushed in pursuit, but, owing to the density of the bush and the darkness, without success. One of the detectives was caught in the throat by a projecting branch, which caused him to fall backwards and inflicted on him several painful scratches and bruises. It was, however, impossible to follow the distillers, as they had evidently got away by some secret path. Giving up the pursuit, the officers returned to the gunyah and took stock of its contents, which consisted of a complete apparatus for distillation, two kegs full of whiskey, and a quantity of liquor in process of manufacture. By this time it was four o'clock, and, being tired out, some slept while one of the party kept guard. The sleepers had to bunk on the ground, with the exception of Christie, who roosted in a large vat. When daylight came, a careful inspection was made of the surroundings and some tracks were picked up. Following these it was found that the distillers used to gain ingress and egress to the place by crawling on all fours through the tangled brushwood. Constables Arthur and Jones then followed the tracks to Love's house, where they found him and brought him back to the gunyah. Other tracks were found which took them in the direction of Tom Delaney's house, but the man was not to be found on the premises. One of the constables was then despatched to Warrnambool for a light waggon in which to remove the still and apparatus. On its arrival the still was placed on the vehicle for transport.

The vehicle, with the party and the prisoner, then proceeded to the township, in which the news of the seizure had been received with some excitement, and their entry into the town was somewhat in the nature of a procession. Love was duly brought up at the Court and convicted. In spite of a strong effort on the part of his counsel to obtain a light sentence, especially on the grounds that he was a man in poor circumstances with a wife and six young children dependent upon him, and had made no resistance to the officers, the Bench inflicted a fine of two hundred and fifty pounds or twelve months' imprisonment. In so doing the Police Magistrate said that the Bench had a public duty to perform, and could not allow any private sympathy for the prisoner's wife and family to interfere with its duty.

Meanwhile Tom Delaney was still at large, and preparations were being made to run him down, when one morning about three weeks afterwards he appeared at daylight at the house of Mr. O'Callaghan, Inspector of Police, in Warrnambool (subsequently Chief Commissioner of Police), and quietly surrendered. This surrender came as a surprise to all concerned, as the man had the reputation of being a somewhat desperate character. However, he evidently did not find the life of a hunted fugitive a pleasant one.

Delaney had been previously fined £25 for smuggling, and he had been caught red-handed in this offence. It was clear he had been carrying on the business of illicit distillation for years, and there was reason to suppose that the men who had been previously convicted and punished were more his dupes than otherwise. In justice to the country the Bench felt they could not give him the option of a fine. He was the principal in the matter, and must receive adequate punishment. That punishment was a sentence of eighteen months' imprisonment.

It may be added that the capture of another still in this district with conviction of the offenders subsequently took place not long afterwards under somewhat similar circumstances, and with that the persons who indulged in the illicit traffic seem to have arrived at the conclusion that the game was not "worth the candle." At all events nothing has been heard of illicit distillation in that district since. Six stills in all were seized, and five persons convicted in connection with them

## CHAPTER XV.

### THE "WIDOW'S" PERAMBULATOR.

IN 1894 Dr. Wollaston learned that illicit spirits were being offered for sale in hotels in the suburbs, and that a smart-looking foreigner carrying sample-bags like a commercial traveller was going round showing samples of spirits in small bottles and asking for orders. This man was offering the liquor at prices which showed no duty could have been paid on it, so that the spirit must either have been illicit, smuggled, or stolen. The Doctor directed Christie to take the matter in hand. The detective accordingly visited various hotels, without any success, but at last found one where the traveller had recently called. The man said that he would call again in a few days. On hearing this, Christie interviewed the landlord, who promised him all the help he could give. Christie requested him, when the traveller called, to give the latter an order for four gallons of whiskey and four of rum to be paid for on delivery. He also arranged for a detective to lodge in the hotel, and shadow the traveller, with a view of finding out where the still was. The liquor was duly ordered and delivery promised the next week. The landlord then invited the "traveller" to have a glass of grog with him, and over this the man said he could supply any quantity of the liquor required once or twice a week. To this the landlord replied that he would take eight or ten gallons a week if sixpence per gallon were knocked off the price, adding: "This you can easily do, as I know the stuff is crooked, but I do not care for that so long as you will supply it according to sample. I come from Ireland myself, from a place where stills are plentiful, and, like all good Irishmen, hate a gauger as I do the devil." This completely put the traveller off his guard, and he at once admitted the stuff was "crooked."

Unfortunately, the detective who had been left to follow the distiller when he left the hotel bungled his job and lost the man, so Christie determined to watch for the delivery of the liquor himself. One day early the following week, when the landlord was alone in the bar, a smartly-dressed young woman came in wheeling a perambulator. She ordered a glass of lemonade and then asked permission to leave two tins of kerosene till her mistress should call for them. The request was acceded to, and the tins placed in a corner of the bar. Next day the traveller called, and after shouting for the publican asked him how he liked the spirit which he had sent him, to which the landlord replied that he had not yet received it. "Oh nonsense," said the man, "my wife left it yesterday. It is in two kerosene tins; I deliver all my liquor that way. You had better pour it into a quarter cask and mix it with other spirits, and then I defy the excise to find out it is ' crooked.' If you will empty the tins I will send for them to-morrow afternoon." This was agreed on, and he left, having previously been paid for the liquor. Unfortunately, for the second time a mistake was made; the publican forgot to tell Christie the man was in the hotel, and he got away without being followed. There was therefore no help for it but to wait and shadow the person who should come for the tins the next day.

Next afternoon Christie was on the look out with the

intention of following the person who came for the empty tins, feeling sure that they would be taken direct to the house where the spirit was manufactured. Whilst so occupied the detective noticed a very attractive- looking young woman, dressed as a widow, with a perambulator, which she left at the door whilst she went into the side parlor. She ordered a glass of lemonade, and then informed him that she had been requested by "her husband" to call for the empty tins. He handed her the tins, when she brought in the perambulator, and, placing the tins therein, covered them over with a kind of mattress. On this she laid a child's head made of wax— a most excellent imitation, with a baby's cap on and a veil over to keep off the flies. She then arranged a cover over all so as to give the exact appearance of a sleeping infant.

Christie had not known that the seeming widow was the person he was on the look-out for, but the landlord came outside and made a signal which had been previously agreed upon. Christie immediately followed her on foot, having in attendance at a little distance a cab, without detection. She continued her way to the Hawthorn bridge. Seeing she was intending to cross the bridge, Christie beckoned up his cab, and jumping into it put on a large Inverness cape and slouch hat, in case the woman might have noticed him before, and told the cabman to drive across the bridge to the top of the opposite hill. After passing over the bridge the woman went up a street and entered a large villa surrounded by an extensive garden, right on the bank of the Yarra. So far satisfied, Christie returned, with the intention of inspecting the house and surroundings after dark.

About eight o'clock he went round the outside fence, got over, and crept up to the villa. There was a light in one of the windows, through which the "widow" and the traveller could be seen having supper together. Thinking they would be occupied for some time he then went to examine a shed in the garden, when he observed the back door of the house open and the man come towards the spot where he was standing. In order to escape detection the officer crept under the fence, and unfortunately for himself fell down a bank which was several feet high, right on his head, on to a ledge which was about one hundred feet above the river. Had he fallen the whole distance he must certainly have been killed, or drowned. He was badly shaken and much bruised. The man heard the noise of the fall, and called out, "Who's there?" and looked about without seeing anybody. Christie lay perfectly still, and the man then returned to the house. Waiting till all was quiet, the detective quickly scrambled up the dangerous cliff and beat a retreat homewards, with the determination to search the place the next day.

There had been in the city several robberies of tobacco, and, under the pretence of searching for the stolen goods, the detective, with two constables, visited the villa the next day and made a search. But though indications were found which showed that the persons were engaged in distillation, no trace of a still itself could be discovered.

The next night, just after dark, Detective Christie established himself on the watch and saw a van drawn up, which was quickly loaded with household effects. This was driven to a house in Abbotsford. Next night the house in Abbotsford was closely watched, and about eight o'clock the man came out carrying a spade and proceeded to the house he had recently vacated. He was seen there to dig up something out of the garden. This object was evidently very heavy, and he had considerable difficulty in carrying it down the steep bank of the river, into which he lowered it.

Next day the officer obtained a boat and rowed up the river till he came to the spot. After searching the bank for some time a wire was detected running down into the water and made fast to the root of a big tree on the bank. Only the most minute search could have revealed its existence. On hauling on this wire a bag came to light which was found to contain a splendid copper worm. Christie then scratched his initials on the worm in a place where they would not be observed and sunk it again in the water.

There was nothing now to be done but keep a close watch over the movements of the suspected couple. For two months a continuous watch was kept, but with no success. During this period they moved twice in the same fashion as before, and the last move was to a house in Richmond. On the opposite side of the street was an empty dwelling, which the detective rented and from there kept a watch. During this watch the woman frequently went out with the perambulator. One of the loads was taken to the publican mentioned before, but although this showed they were again engaged in the trade it was determined to wait till the still could be found in actual working.

One night a heavy fire had been kept up all night in the house under surveillance, and a great flow of water came from the place. The detective considered that the time had come to search the place. Next day was Sunday, and at dusk the place was kept under watch by Christie, with two constables. Shortly after dusk the man was seen to enter the house, and Christie immediately went to the front door and knocked. The door was slightly opened, and the man was heard to say: "Who's there? Is that you, Annie?" Christie, on the door being opened, had pushed in his foot and called out: "I am Detective Christie. You must surrender." The man endeavoured to close the door, which, however, was forced open by the detective, with whom the man immediately grappled. He proved himself a powerful opponent and fought desperately. Christie drew his revolver, bailed the man up in a corner of the room with his hands up, and, keeping his weapon pointed at him, opened the door and called out for the constables, who immediately took charge of the captured man.

An inspection of the interior disclosed a complete distillery in full working order—mash tubs with liquor in various stages of preparation, the worm being the one which had been in the river, and still bore the detective's initials. Large quantities of flavouring essences and compounds were found, which were used to give the distinctive flavour and colour of whiskey, brandy, gin, etc., and the silent spirit manufactures. There was also found a revolver fully loaded, and a heavy life preserver, which was placed just behind the front door, ready evidently for emergencies. The man afterwards confessed that his object in struggling so when arrested was to get at this preserver, and he would certainly have settled his captor if he could have reached it.

## DETECTIVE CHRISTIE.

The prisoner was shortly afterwards tried and convicted. He was fined £200 or twelve months' imprisonment, and the whole contents of the house, including furniture, forfeited.

## CHAPTER XVI.

### THE COFFIN TRICK.

HERE is another of the various devices used in the conveyance of illicit spirits. One Sunday night Christie was passing St. Patrick's Cathedral, in East Melbourne, when his notice was attracted by a man who was carrying what looked like a child's coffin on his shoulder draped with black cloth. This man passed close to the detective, who, seeing his face under the gaslight, thought he recognised him as a criminal who was a notorious "moonlighter." He had now the appearance of an undertaker going to deliver a child's coffin. Christie shadowed him down to a house in a neighbouring street, and, having obtained the assistance of two constables, that night went there, but found the gates locked. The detective was hoisted over the back fence and found everything in darkness. He then burst in the back door, and inside caught the inmate actually at work at a still. He immediately covered the man with his revolver and ordered him to throw up his hands, which the man did, saying, "All right, Mr. Christie, I give in." The distiller was marched off to the lock-up. In due course, he was found guilty and a fine of £150 inflicted, or twelve months' imprisonment. After conviction he asked Christie who had given the information about himself, and when told how he had been suspected, he replied, "Well, I thought the devil himself would not tumble to the coffin trick. It was merely two kerosene tins fastened end to end and wrapped in the black table-cover you found on the table in the kitchen."

## A BOGUS ILLICIT STILL.

The Department of Trade and Customs offers a very substantial reward for information leading to the capture of a still and the conviction of offenders. In a few instances, however, the Department has been deceived and "got at" by bogus informers. One of these cases was in relation to an alleged illicit still. An official notice stated a reward of £100 would be paid for the capture of an illicit still and apprehension and subsequent conviction of the distillers. There were two men who were "chums," but had for some time been living on their wits, and at last were reduced to great extremities to support themselves. A brilliant idea, however, occurred to one of them by which the two could make a "rise." Bill, the cleverer of the two, being a man who formerly occupied a superior position and was somewhat of a lawyer, suggested to his mate that if they could manage to scrape together the old boiler and tubing which was all that was necessary, and constitute a "still" in the legal sense, they could set one up in a fashion and work it a bit, not with a view to making spirits and selling them, but in order to obtain the reward offered for detection. Bill pointed out that all that was required was that they should pretend to work the still and that one of the partners should then "split"—information for which the £100 was offered. Further, that as it was winter, and they were literally on their beam-ends, it would be no hardship for either of them to do three months or so in gaol, and when he came out the half of the reward, fifty pounds, would be waiting for him, which would be a pretty fair return for a compulsory residence in the "Queen's Hotel" in comfortable quarters, at the worst season of the year.

To this Bill's partner, Jim, agreed as a very feasible plan. The men, with the proverbial honor amongst thieves which is said to exist, had confidence in each other, having been associated together for some time. Assured that neither would slip the other up, and as Bill was the sharpest and most presentable of the two, it was agreed that he should give the information, whilst Jim should do the inevitable stretch in the "jug." Accordingly they set up a rough still in the bush in the neighbourhood of a country town not far from Melbourne. They then got some grain and made some stuff which could pass as technically "spirit," and when all their preparations were ready, Bill went off to Melbourne to give his mate away. The exact day and hour when the detectives were to come upon the still were agreed on between them, and, at this hour, Jim was to have a big fire going and be apparently busily engaged in the manufacture of spirit.

Bill then appeared at the office desiring to see the Detective-Inspector and duly interviewed that official. The Detective-Inspector, well pleased at the prospect of making such an important seizure as the information seemed to promise, got his men together and set out just before daylight. Bill had stipulated, however, that while he would guide them to the locality and show the precise spot in which the still was, he himself was to remain hidden, because if it should be discovered that he had given his mate away the consequences to himself would be most serious.

The party cautiously approached the spot, and soon

they saw the gleam of fire in a clump of tangled scrub, and, on approaching nearer, saw a bush "humpy" with a fireplace composed of rough stones, in which a big fire was blazing, and a man to all appearances hard at work attending to the heating of liquid, whilst a strong smell of spirit pervaded the air. The detectives surrounded the hut, revolvers were drawn, and, crying in a loud voice: "Hands up! You are our prisoner," they forced an entrance. The distiller was promptly handcuffed, seemingly utterly "flabbergasted" by his sudden arrest. He growled out something to the effect that if he had known the "encarmined" detectives were about he would have prepared a hot reception for them. Having secured their prisoner, the officers proceeded to investigate the extent of their capture, but were intensely disgusted and disappointed to find that instead of being a fully-equipped still of the largest capacity, and with all necessary appliances, which they had been led to expect, it was only one of the most make-shift kind, hardly to be dignified by the name of still at all. They determined, however, to make the best of it, and marched their prisoner off, the man preserving a sullen silence all the time. Seeing it was such a small affair the officers lost much of their interest in the seizure. Jim was brought up in a day or two and promptly fined £50, with the alternative of three months' imprisonment. Bill turned up promptly on the day his mate had been convicted and demanded his money. The officials were very much disinclined to pay the full amount of £100 for such a meagre capture, and demurred to paying over the sovereigns. However, seeing the precise tones of the official notice which promised the reward without any qualification, after a few days' hesitation, Bill got the money.

It appeared that he was loyal to his mate and duly kept for him and handed over the fifty "quid" which was the latter's share of the spoil. The officials, however, when they made the tardy discovery that they had been hoaxed, at once withdrew the existing notice and substituted one for it which contained certain restrictions and conditions which would prevent their being again taken in.

## CHAPTER XVII.

### WOMEN SMUGGLERS.

IT is a trite saying that in regard to Customs duties women possess no conscience. There exist some men perhaps who under no possible circumstances would desire to escape the payment of duties levied according to law; but as to women, it would seem as if few exceptions can be made. The officials declare that women of all classes "do" the Customs. The famous signal of Nelson which the Customs officers read, "England expects that every man will *pay* his duty," has no weight with them. They cannot be made to see that the avoidance of the payment of dues which are levied according to law is an obligation.

Many men are mean enough, and often the wealthier they are the more they object to part with more coin through the Customs than they can be compelled to, but it is women who as a rule show the greatest disinclination to obey the law. It is on record as an example of what men will sometimes do to escape the payment of a small sum, that a travelling nobleman who was staying at Government House, and who as a matter of courtesy was furnished by the Victorian Government with a free pass on the railways, wrote to the Head of the Customs, on Government paper and under a frank stamp, complaining that he had been called upon to pay duty on a pair of slippers which had been sent to him from England, and expressed his indignation at such a demand being made upon him. Now, the amount of the duty involved was the large sum of two and sixpence! The Head was so lost to every sense of what the circumstances required, and so regardless of the risk that he ran of being excluded in future from those select functions at Government House to which he had hitherto been accorded the right of entree, that he actually ventured to inform "my lord" in courteous terms that the money was properly due, and that his lordship could not get the slippers till he paid up. Moreover, that he had better pay up sharply, or they would be taken possession of and sold. The peer was further informed that should, however, the sale take place and any surplus was left of the proceeds after payment of the duty and all expenses connected with the sale, such balance, after due presentation of the necessary documents and compliance with the prescribed formalities, including evidence of ownership of the slippers being vested in himself, the Department would be prepared to pay the same over to him. In fact the peer was actually snubbed!

Sealskins and furs above all things seem to have an irresistible fascination for some of the fair sex, and their ordinary attraction is considerably increased if in addition the charm of having escaped the payment of heavy duty is added. The motives which induce persons to give such information have been referred to elsewhere. Sometimes it is envy, jealousy, or revenge; more often it is the temptation to secure the handsome reward which the Department always pays to an informer. Many persons in Australia who have suffered at the hands of the Customs would be startled if they could learn the names of the people who had betrayed them. Confidential clerks; intimate female friends; domestic servants; all figure on the list. The information is often given only with the greatest precaution.

In one case the Head received a perfumed note, evidently written by a woman of some education, which expressed a desire on the part of the writer to have a private interview with him, but not in his office. Such missives were, however, no particular novelty. No notice was taken of the first letter, but a second was soon afterwards received. It had, however, apparently occurred to the writer that the reason she had received no answer to her first communication was that a trap was suspected, and in her second letter the writer made it clear that the interview she sought was of a business nature entirely, in which sentiment would have no place, and that it was in her power to impart some information as to contemplated smuggling. Consequently the Chief sent an acknowledgement of the second letter, saying the Department would be glad to have any information of a reliable character that could be supplied, and that he proposed to send his confidential Inspector, Mr. Christie, to interview the lady. An answer to this letter was, however, soon received, in which the lady said that she preferred for many reasons to deal with the Head of the Department alone. After consideration and consultation with Christie it was decided to invite the lady to visit the office to interview the Chief. To this invitation the lady replied in a sarcastic vein, intimating that she was not quite such a fool as to accept. She wound up by saying that unless her first request was granted, the offer was to be considered as entirely "off." This communication looked like business, and as if the lady might really have something important to give away. So an appointment was made for the Flinders Street Railway station.

At the time appointed the Chief was duly on hand,

and the writer of the letters disclosed herself as a very charming-looking girl of about twenty, attractively dressed and of ladylike manners. He soon came to the point, and desired her as briefly and clearly as she could to make her statement, which he promised her should be kept entirely secret. There was, however, some difficulty in getting her to speak out, and a railway station was perhaps not the best of places to receive confidences from such fair lips. However, the Chief soon had an inspiration as to the best way of getting the girl to make a clean breast of it. He suggested to his fair interviewer that an adjournment for lunch would be advisable, when she could speak freely. After lunch had been duly disposed of, the girl told all she knew to her father-confessor. A scheme had come to her ears which had been concocted by two women of her acquaintance in good positions "to run" some most valuable furs and other garments from the mail steamer then shortly expected. Christie was instructed and the culprits caught in *flagrante delicto*. The whole consignment was confiscated and the two dames fined £100 each. The girl had one last private interview with the Chief, when a weighty bag of golden sovereigns was passed by him to her.

In another important case the game was "blown on" by a maid in the employ of the lady concerned. This girl, in the course of her waiting at table, had heard chance remarks which convinced her something was in the wind. Accordingly she laid herself out to pick up all the information she could. This girl knew how substantial was the reward paid by a generous Government to those who assisted in collecting their just dues. Moreover, the girl had a lover whom she wished to marry, but hitherto circumstances had not been altogether propitious for want of the needful. Hence the hundred pounds which she saw before her eyes was a powerful temptation to her. Having thus made up her mind to "split," the rest was easy. The maid had a female confederate. The latter called on the Head; Christie was sent for, and a very pretty little game was disclosed. The mistress was a lady of means who lived in very good style in St. Kilda and had an intimate lady friend. The scheme was this. The husband of the mistress of the house had gone to England, and was about to return. Numerous and expensive articles of feminine attire were to be bought in London and on the Continent and brought out as portion of his luggage. The two ladies were to go to Adelaide and meet the steamer there and come back in her as passengers, and whilst on board take possession of the new clothes and land at Port Melbourne wearing the most valuable and bring ashore the rest as ordinary wearing apparel not subject to duty. This scheme was successfully carried out up to the landing at Port Melbourne. But here trouble commenced, and the scheme was wrecked. Christie and his assistants were on the watch. The mistress gaily tripped down the gangway to the wharf, closely followed by her friend, and walked to the end of the pier, where her carriage was in waiting. One was wearing a magnificent sealskin mantle and rather singularly a sealskin cape over the shoulders of it, whilst the other wore a new sealskin cape of the best quality and style. The officers followed the carriage in a cab to the residence at St. Kilda. Having obtained an interview with the mistress, she was asked if she had brought any dutiable goods ashore. She emphatically denied having done so, but when she was notified that the officers must then search the house, the sealskin cape and mantle were produced, but the lady said they were old garments. Unfortunately for her, however, the Customs officers gain considerable knowledge of what relates to these articles, and are able to tell a new garment from one that has been worn. A glance at the furs showed the garments were new. Christie then formally seized the articles, and after some further pressure the lady called her husband, who admitted that he had brought out the furs with him. He added, however, that he had no other dutiable goods with him. An unfortunate falsehood, for the officers knew better, and he only increased his punishment. The detectives insisted on searching his trunks, and found in them a varied assortment of dutiable articles.

So far so good. But there was the lady friend to be accounted for. This person had been kept under surveillance for some days in the hope that by her means something more would come to light, and one day she was followed to Spencer Street, where she took a ticket for the express to Sydney. Christie was there, but was somewhat puzzled, as the lady's hair seemed a different tint from what it had been when she landed at Port Melbourne, and he was consequently rather dubious as to her identity. But he boldly accosted the lady, asking her to accompany him into the waiting-room with her belongings. She was highly indignant, and expressed her opinion in no unmeasured terms at the "outrage" which was being committed on her. But the detective was persistent. When in the room he felt and opened a railway cushion she had with her, and within was found a fine sealskin jacket carefully folded up. The lady said it was only an old one, and she carried it that way for convenience sake. The detective, however, was sceptical, and desired her to accompany him to the Customs House, whither she went with very ill grace. But here a difficulty presented itself. It was all very well for the detective to hunt down illicit stills and moonlighters, but to investigate the intricacies of feminine apparel in actual use was a task beyond his limit. The lady would not own up and would not disgorge. But the emergency was soon grappled with. The housekeeper's wife was sent for, the room was given up to the women, and a search disclosed a handsome and valuable necklace and a small costly gold watch and pendant.

As a result the whole of the seizure was forfeited to the Crown and sold for the benefit of the revenue, and the two women had to pay in addition a fine of £100 each. The spoils were catalogued and found to be not only the very rich and expensive furs already mentioned and the jewellery, but also several costumes, blouses, veils, boots and shoes, gloves, perfumes, hair-wash and hair-dye, intended for the use of society dames, and, last but not least, "improvers." It may be added the subsequent sale created considerable interest amongst society women, and the Department netted a considerable amount over the transaction. The maid was duly remunerated and her swain made a happy man, and let us hope they lived happily ever afterwards.

Apropos of letters, it is singular how these seem to turn up unexpectedly to disclose matters which but for them would be otherwise hidden. For instance, at one time there was a considerable amount of smuggling over the New South Wales border into the broken and mountainous country of Gippsland, and much trouble given to the Customs and Police in consequence. In one case, the principal smuggler was strongly suspected, but he could not be caught, nor could any reliable evidence be obtained against him. A sagacious police constable, however, once on his lonely patrol through the forest came across a bit of dirty and crumpled paper which his curiosity led him to inspect, as he observed it had been written on, and the sight of an apparent letter in that locality was a rarety. He perused it at the end of a stick, not caring to handle it, and then forwarded it on to headquarters, with a warning in the corner to be careful in the handling of the contents. On perusal, with the assistance of a paper-knife and a little eau de cologne, the contents proved to be a communication from one of the smuggler's pals, disclosing a plan for running some cattle across. Christie was duly instructed, and the parties "nabbed" and convicted.

In another instance the "bowl out" was rather amusing. A certain Lady Blank had ordered a dress, to be worn at the approaching Cup races in Melbourne. It was invoiced at, say, ten pounds, but the Customs officials saw at a glance from its make and material, and also from the fact of its coming from a celebrated and worldwide known "builder" of feminine attire in Paris, its cost was certainly very much over that amount. The lady was accordingly told that the value placed upon it could not be accepted, and that the duty alone would be more than the stated value of the frock. She was very angry at this demand and indignant at the action of the officers, and intimated that she would interview the Head of the Department and see that their insolence was properly dealt with. Accordingly she called upon the Chief, stating her grievance, and demanded redress. He was all smiles and courtesy; sympathised with the lady and soothed her ruffled susceptibilities in his very best manner. He assured her that it was only necessary for her to produce some evidence that the price to be paid for the "confection" was only what she stated it to be, and it would be accepted at once. The lady calmed down, and from her peggy-bag brought forth various bills and documents, which she handed over to him for perusal as supporting her contention. One of these documents was a letter written in French from the maker of the article. Now, whether the lady's knowledge of the French language was not equal to the charms she undoubtedly possessed, or whether in the excitement of the moment she had forgotten the exact purport of the letter in question, we know not. Suffice it to say, however, that on perusal the letter read to the effect that the invoice or bill which had been originally produced to the Customs officials was only prepared and forwarded so as to enable the recipient to hoodwink the Customs and escape the payment of duty, and that the real price the maker of the frock expected to receive was very much higher than the sum mentioned in the fictitious bill, and the writer would be glad to have a remittance of that amount. The Chief translated the document to the lady, who had not then a word to say for herself, and the usual consequences of course inevitably followed.

On one occasion a man having the appearance of an

American traveller, carrying a bag apparently containing samples, strolled into an hotel at the seaside and entered the private parlour, where the buxom and not unattractive landlady happened to be present. The stranger, being a personable man with pleasant manners, and the lady not being coy and apparently not offended at the evident admiration with which the American regarded her, soon grew chatty and made herself very agreeable. At the invitation of the stranger a glass of wine was partaken of, after which the traveller produced some cigars, which he informed the landlady were samples of what he had to dispose of. She inquired the price, but on hearing what was asked for them said: "Oh, that is too much; I can get imported cigars and good ones too for much less."

To this the traveller replied that he would be glad to purchase as well as sell, and if she could put him in the way of getting any good cigars cheap he would be much obliged.

"I can let you have a quantity of good cigars at six pounds the thousand," said the landlady.

"You must then be smuggling them," answered the traveller, "to be able to afford to sell them at that rate."

She smiled knowingly, replying: "You can bet your bottom dollar I do. The Customs officers are easily done; they can't see a hole as big as a haystack."

"Well, they always seem to me pretty sharp when I am about," said the traveller. "How many cigars can you let me have at the price you mentioned?"

"If you will come here on Good Friday I will have 4,000 cigars for you," replied the landlady.

The traveller agreed to take that quantity, at the same

time warning her to be careful of the Customs officials; but she did not seem much afraid of them, as she remarked she could always manage them all right, adding that the only one she was at all afraid of was Christie, and enquiring if the traveller knew him.

"Oh yes," he answered. "I have seen him, but do not fancy he is up to much. Anyway, those bright eyes of yours would fix him up to rights if you ever came across him."

"There is a brewer's traveller, Mr. Lyons, I know, who is going to bring him in here some day, so that I may be introduced and get to know him, when I will do my best to get round him."

"Well, be careful you are not found out and take care of yourself. So long." With these words the traveller departed.

On Good Friday Christie—who was, of course, the pretended traveller of the previous occasion—walked into the bar-parlour of the hotel, and the landlady appeared and recognised him at once, saying: "I have got those cigars for you I promised the other day. I did the Customs officers beautifully. They had no suspicion of me."

At these words Christie pretended to be puzzled, and did not apparently understand what cigars she meant.

"Are you not the traveller who was in here a few days ago?"

"No," said Christie; "I am to meet Mr. Lyons here, as he asked me to meet him here to-day. My name is Inspector Christie. Who are the Customs officers you have done so beautifully?"

## WOMEN SMUGGLERS.

"I was only joking," replied the lady, realising she had made a mistake.

"Well, I do not like jokes of that kind at the expense of my brother officers, and after your remarks I must search your premises to see if you have any smuggled cigars in the place."

He then called the constables he had in attendance outside and placed them at all the exits, keeping a sharp eye on the landlady. He observed her whisper to the barman, who immediately proceeded quickly to her bedroom. The detective followed at once, and found the door of the room locked inside, but, by a vigorous thrust with the whole weight of his body, burst it open and found the man alongside his mistress's bed, with a cornsack in his hand. On searching the bed, the four thousand cigars in boxes were found concealed under the bedclothes.

A further search revealed petticoats and feminine garments of a more intimate nature, which had been specially contrived for smuggling boxes of cigars or bottles of spirits. Rows of deep pockets were fixed around the garments, which were made of stout material, into which the boxes or bottles could be slipped and so carried ashore. Women knew there would be no personal search except by women-searchers, and that such rarely takes place, and only in cases of the gravest suspicion, consequently female smugglers concealing goods in this manner often escape detection.

The landlady was prosecuted and fined £50, and the cigars forfeited to the Crown.

## CHAPTER XVIII.

## THE GENTLE ART OF "CRIMPING."

CRIMPING ("shanghaing" as it is sometimes termed), used to be very rife at the Port of Melbourne for many years, and the place had a bad reputation in this respect owing to the evil practices of a number of notorious crimps, who would stick at nothing to make money out of the unfortunate sailors. The evil, however, was completely suppressed when Dr. Wollaston became Permanent Head of the Department of Trade and Customs, which had control of all shipping and marine matters. Acting under his instructions, the crimps were relentlessly pursued by the officers of the department and no trouble or expense spared to suppress them. As a result every one of them was ultimately convicted and served a sentence in gaol. The officials who were more especially instrumental in carrying out this duty were Captain Nichol, Overseer of Seamen, (a former P. & O. Company's officer) and Inspector Christie. The first-named, being a sailor himself, was on that account able to render most intelligent and valuable service.

In old days, when sailing vessels formed the bulk of shipping visiting the port, they would make hardly more than one voyage in the twelve months, owing to the length of time they would be detained in harbour waiting for orders. On arrival the crew would have a considerable amount of pay due to each, and if they left the ship without being legally discharged all this money would be forfeited. The ship would thus have had their services practically for nothing, with the exception of the one month's pay which each man received when he shipped, by means of what is known as an "advance note." As articles are usually signed for three years, during the detention of the ship the men's wages would run on, and there would be in addition the cost of keeping them in food. If, however, the men deserted or "ran," not only were the wages saved to the ship, but also the expense of maintenance. Naturally enough, masters of ships who wished to show good returns were not averse to the men leaving the vessel without legal sanction. Indeed, many would actually give the crimps a bonus on each man they enticed on shore and sent off in other vessels.

It can easily be imagined that the temptation to have a good spree on shore after the privations and monotony of a long voyage at sea would be too much for the men, who, once in the clutches of the crimps, were kept in a muddled state till they were shipped again.

The unfortunate sailors were fleeced by the crimps in many ways, and by many indirect methods. In the first place, a master who was seeking a crew would pay a bonus for each man brought on board by the crimp. At a time when seamen were very scarce, such a bonus would run as high as £5 per head. Next, when a seaman signed on, he was entitled to receive an advance note, which is a document authorising the bearer to receive one month's wages from the local agent of the ship as soon as she had cleared the port. The object of this advance note was that each man might have a little money to buy clothes, etc. But the crimp would get hold of it, give the sailor a few miserable "duds," and, having made him tipsy, send him to sea and himself draw the money. Most of the amount would be clear profit to him and a direct robbery of the sailor. When the wages were, say, £10 a month and an advance note was given for one month's pay, the crimp could easily net eight pounds by "doing" the sailor. If, besides this, he got a tip for enticing the man ashore from his other ship in the first instance, it would not be difficult to make ten pounds a head on each man going through his hands, and, as the number of seamen required for an oversea ship would number from fifteen to forty men, it can easily be understood that the gains the crimps made were considerable.

Sometimes, however, when men were scarce, and indeed not to be got at all, and the ship was only to make a short stay in port, the desire of the master would be all the other way. He would wish to keep his men, so as to avoid paying higher wages to a new crew or the delay to his ship whilst waiting a crew. When foreign wages were, say, four pounds a month and colonial rates ten pounds, the inducement to a crew which had shipped in England to "run" would be very great indeed, even if they did lose their accrued wages. In such circumstances, in order to prevent the men slipping ashore, great vigilance would have to be exercised by the officers of the ship. The vessel would be out in the bay at anchor, and no person would be allowed on board without their permission, and no seaman who could not be trusted to return, would be allowed to go ashore. Particularly was this the case with American ships. Of course all deserters are liable to be arrested and put on

## THE GENTLE ART OF "CRIMPING." 163

board the vessel they belong to by force, but when the crimps were in full swing conducting their nefarious business, such arrests were infrequent and difficult to effect. Yet after the crimps were suppressed it was comparatively easy to find any men who had "run," especially if they were foreigners. Men knew it was useless to attempt to escape, as they would soon be picked up by the police and sent on board.

On one occasion, two sailors tried to make use of the law to obtain their retention in Victoria. The *Mary Jane* barque, of Boston, U.S.A., was lying in Hobson's Bay ready for sea, when two of the sailors got ashore by stowing themselves in a bum boat. Immediately they landed they went to Mr. James Daly Emmerson, a lawyer. The latter saw at a glance they were "shell-backs," and asked them what they wanted. They asked what fee was to be paid for advice. They were informed one guinea, which amount was immediately handed over. They then went on to ask the solicitor if it were the case that in Victoria a wife who knew her husband was going out of the State and leaving her without means for her support could obtain a warrant for his arrest and have him detained. They were told that such was the case. The men seemed satisfied with this and left.

About nine o'clock the same evening the solicitor referred to was walking down the street, when he observed lights in the front-room of the local parsonage and a cab standing at the gate. He asked the cabman what was going on. Cabby replied: "Shure, *you* ought to know, sorr."

"Why should I know?" said the lawyer, who then learnt that it was this cabman who had driven the seamen to his house earlier in the evening and thence to a local public house, where the men had each picked up a fair but frail one who, for a consideration, and unlimited liquors, was willing to go through the marriage ceremony with him, and then to lay an information next morning against the husband and obtain his detention.

The two couples were at that moment being married. The next evening the solicitor was at a lodge meeting, when a very tall brother, evidently a Yankee, came and introduced himself as the master of the *Mary Jane*. Then he said: "Well, Brother Emmerson, you thought you had done me a nice trick by getting two of my sailors to get spliced to two street "whalers." But I have weathered on you to rights, I guess. I got the women to ship, one as a stewardess and the other as cook. I have taken the wind out of your sails, and, besides, have done a Christian act by giving the women a chance to reform." The ship duly sailed with the men and their brides, but what subsequently happened history does not record, and perhaps that is just as well.

The notorious crimps at the Port of Melbourne rejoiced in various nicknames, such as "Blueskin," "The Ghost," "Flash Jack," "Blue Nose," and "Jack Sheppard." One was a woman who rejoiced in the classic name of Cassandra, and had the pseudonym of "Port Wine Mary Anne," so called from a large birth-mark on her face. She was well known personally or by repute all over the world amongst deep-sea sailors. The dodges and tricks practised by these persons were of infinite variety, not to mention many other actions which were pure villainies.

Late one night the master of the well-known Greens' ship the *Renown,* which was due to sail at daylight the next morning, called on Christie and informed him that six of his crew had deserted since tea-time, one of them a big nigger, and that it was of the utmost importance to the ship to recover them. It was evident, therefore, that no time was to be lost. The assistance of half-a-dozen constables was obtained, and the whole party then drove down to Port Melbourne, where was situated a public house kept by the notorious "Blueskin," also known as "King of the Crimps." Some of the police were placed to watch the "pub" back and front, whilst the skipper, with Christie and a constable, knocked at the front door. Lights were plainly visible. As soon, however, as the knock was given all lights were "doused," and presently an upstairs window was thrown up and the head of the virtuous "Blueskin" protruded. The latter expressed his surprise at being disturbed so late at night. What he said, however, did not make much impression on his hearers, who told him that if he did not open his door at once, it would be forced open, and, almost simultaneously, a ship's bell was heard to ring twice inside the building. The fact of the bell being thus rung was evidence to those acquainted with the ways of the crimps that the men wanted were on the premises, and were probably concealed in some hiding-places known to exist in the building.

These hiding-places were very cleverly constructed, whole sides of some of the bedrooms being partitioned off, having cunningly constructed spring doors in the partitions, which doors could not be detected except after careful inspection, inch by inch, of the whole of the partition. Inside was a ladder running up to the roof. When the alarm bell rang once, if the runaways were in the bedrooms, they would be hustled by the crimps' assistants behind the partitions, and if the bell rang twice, it meant the men were to be taken up to the roof, where they would be able to drop down into the street behind or over other houses, and so escape. In this instance, only three of the deserters got up to the roof, one of whom was the darkey. They clambered over the neighbouring housetops and were seen by one of the watching constables to be descending into a back yard. But before they could be intercepted by him they managed to get away. The constable immediately ran into the public house and informed Christie, who, leaving the other police to guard the hotel and search for the other three men, jumped into the waggonette which had brought the party from town, and, driving it himself, went round into the street into which the three men had probably got by this time. He was fortunate enough to see them bolting up the street as hard as they could go. He whipped up his horse, and when he got abreast of them, pretending to be the cabman, sang out to them: "The police are after you, boys; jump up quick, and I'll get you away." They got in, and were driven round to the police station, before the passengers could realise that they had been trapped. He marched the three men into the watchhouse, where they were temporarily locked up. He then returned as quickly as possible to the "pub," where he found that the other three men had been discovered "three sheets in the wind," and consequently too drunk to get up on the roof in time to escape. The whole six, under police escort, were conveyed aboard the *Renown,* which duly sailed at the advertised time.

In another case, the master of one of the famous clipper ships which used to trade to Australia was a crack boxer, and always contrived to have as a member of his crew a man who could also "put up his dukes." This clipper was lying out in the stream, when the skipper found to his disgust that the fighting black, who was his second cook, had deserted. The master knew all the principal professional fighting men in Melbourne, and immediately went on shore to obtain a man to take the place of the deserter. He went to the public house of "Blueskin," informed him of his loss, and desired him to set to work to obtain another fighting sailor. The captain of the clipper specially mentioned "Black Albert." This individual was a well-known boxer, and had fought with Peter Newton, a famous pugilist of his time. He added that he would give the crimp five pounds for his trouble. "Blueskin" at once accepted the task. In undertaking this, however, he found that he had promised more than he could fulfil, for when the gang attempted to inveigle the black down to the "pub," they saw he was too fly for them. Being an old "shell back," he evidently smelt a rat. Failing this man, they then tried their wits upon a noted pugilist, named Jimmy Shannon, whom they invited to come down to the hotel in the evening for the ostensible purpose of arranging for an exhibition of boxing which was to take place in the lounge, promising him five pounds for his night's work. Jimmy willingly accepted the invitation. He duly turned up the next evening and discussed the arrangements for the pretended exhibition. Whilst his attention was otherwise engaged, a drug was skilfully added to his liquor, with the result that he soon became helpless. The gang then removed him to a room known as the "dead house," till he could be carried off in an apparently drunken condition to be shipped. There they took from him his watch, chain and money, and then in a most artistic fashion blacked all those portions of his body which were not covered by his clothes, so that he would look like a nigger and pass for "Black Albert." They would thus be able to get the five pounds promised by the master. Late the same evening poor Jimmy was taken, still unconscious, to the ship by "The Ghost" and "Blueskin," and, on arrival, was dumped down in the forecastle. The chief officer was at the gangway, and told the skipper that the nigger had been brought off by the crimp. The captain accordingly handed over the promised five pounds and the advance note, and the rascals departed, chuckling over the success of their plot.

Another instance well illustrates the simple manner in which poor Jack allows such sharks and harpies to prey upon and ill-treat him. Three seamen were on one occasion "shanghaied" on board a vessel bound to England and back. On the voyage these men determined that they would return to Melbourne in company and take their revenge upon the crimp. As luck would have it, the first night they returned to Port Melbourne they ran up against "Blueskin" himself. They professed the greatest pleasure at meeting him, ignoring all that had taken place, and after a little talk invited the crimp to a neighbouring "pub" to have a drink. "Blueskin," however, who well knew who the men were and suspected their intentions, put them off on the plea he was busy just then, but invited them all to come up to his hotel at eight o'clock, when he would be glad to "shout" for them, and give them a good time generally. The men, still with their vengeance in view, willingly agreed, and were duly on hand, anxiously awaiting the crimp's advent for the purpose of taking it out of him. "The Ghost," Blueskin's principal aide-de-camp, had however been notified by his master that the men were coming, and directed to keep the men amused and to ply them freely with drink in the interval. The men were nothing loath to drink at his expense, and thus had no hesitation in filling themselves up on the drugged liquor supplied. By the time "Blueskin" appeared on the scene, the three were all blind-drunk and helpless. Now, it so happened that the gang had an order to find some men for a ship that was to sail at daylight the next morning. The trio of revenge-seekers were accordingly carried out of the back door, driven to the shore, and taken off to the ship, where they were bundled into the forecastle, there to dream of revenge and, on waking, find that their experience of it had been by no means sweet.

## CHAPTER XIX.

## OPIUM SMUGGLING AND OPIUM SWINDLERS.

A WELL-KNOWN authority has stated that "for ways that are dark and tricks that are vain the heathen Chinee is peculiar," and the correctness of this statement is well borne out by the Customs officials of Australia, who have, for many years, had to contend with the cunning and ingenuity of celestials in their attempts to evade the heavy duties on opium. Though the importation of opium has, of late years, been entirely prohibited by the Federal Government, such prohibition has rather increased than otherwise the fertility of the Chinese imagination and ingenuity in the attempt to evade the vigilance of the officers and to smuggle it into the Commonwealth. The Chinese, many of whom have become habitual opium-smokers, are incapable of doing without it, and will give any price and use any device to procure it.

The effect of prohibition has been to very largely increase the gains of the smugglers when successful, and so remunerative has become the trade to those who manage to run any quantity of the stuff, that many white people also have become smugglers of the article and thus rendered the attempt to entirely suppress its importation increasingly difficult. Up to the time of the prohibition, the attempts to smuggle were, as a rule, confined almost entirely to Chinese, and that only by vessels coming direct from the East. But now, when so much larger profits await the successful smuggler, the article is sent by

*From "The Australasian," June 7, 1890.*

### Smugglers and their Dodges.
*(see back)*

Facing page 170]

## SMUGGLERS AND THEIR DODGES.

(See Illustration)

1.—The Waistcoat with 170 inside pockets for Watch Smuggling.

2.—The Dummy Umbrella, used for "Ring Sneaking" over the Border.

3.—Chinese False-Bottomed Box, showing smuggled Opium in skins.

4.—Opium Belt put round the Chest.

5.—The Hollow-Backed Jewel Smuggler. (The lines show the box held in position by the braces).

6.—The "Improver" Dodge. (When in fashion wearers had to be watched carefully).

7.—Customs' Officer: "John, you welly fat." John: "Don't touchee me, me got heart disease." (He was suffering from two opium belts round his chest).

8.—Disguises of a Customs' Detective.

9.—Detective (to returned Colonist who has brought out a few things for his tall friend Brown): "All those clothes yours? You must have shrunk a good deal on the voyage, Sir."

10.—Customs' Officer (after plunging his bayonet through the false bottom of Ah Sin's clothes box, and finding the point covered with opium): "Whose box this?" Chorus of Celestials: "No savee!"

11.—A Ruse Lately Played. Six Chinamen draw off the two Customs watchers, while the seventh sneaks a big swag of cigars ashore.

12.—On the Overland Trip from Sydney. Suspicious Detective: "I beg your pardon, Sir. Hullo! What's that in your hat?" (It was a diamond tiara.)

all kinds of devious ways to Australia, as it pays well to send the opium *via* England or America. When it is remembered that a pound of the stuff can be packed into a receptacle not three inches square, and that when successfully landed it will fetch £10, if of superior quality, it is very evident that without a personal search of every person arriving in Australia from abroad, obviously impossible, its detection can never be altogether complete.

Many years ago, when the duty on opium was 20/- per lb. and the Chinese population of Victoria much larger than it is now, it became evident to the Customs authorities that large quantities of the stuff were being used in the colony on which the duty had not been paid. The officials were at their wits' end to discover how the smuggling was managed, but did not find out until the offer of a very large reward induced an informer (a Chinese) to show how the evasion of duty was effected.

The means adopted were as follows:—During the time when the new season's tea arrives the Customs sheds are filled up with boxes all marked with Chinese hieroglyphics and each bearing a strong family resemblance to the other. The idea occurred to the smugglers that by placing the opium tins in the middle of the chests, surrounded and concealed by tea, they would escape detection, but as it was the practice of the officers who examined importations to have cases opened haphazard for the purpose of inspection, it was necessary to place the opium in some only of the chests, and to so manage that none of the latter were selected for inspection. The boxes which did contain opium were marked with a Chinese ideograph which signified "dirt." Though such a mark would convey nothing to the western eye, a

Chinese would immediately detect it. Consequently when the tea chests were piled in immense stacks, and the examining officers would point out the particular boxes they wished open, it was easy for a Chinese labourer ostensibly to pick out the particular ones indicated by the officer, but contrive that none bearing the distinguishing mark should be opened. By this means a most lucrative trade sprung up and fortunes were made by Chinese.

When, however, this information was obtained, prompt action was taken by the authorities. The cargo of each incoming tea ship was carefully inspected, with the result that £70,000 worth of opium was seized. The two officers principally active in the detection received a thousand pounds each from the Government for ability shown in the case, and the informers a very large reward. While wholesale importations were thus stopped, yet considerable quantities would still continue to come in through all kinds of channels and in all kinds of ways, and, indeed, still do so.

Besides the well-known devices of false bottoms to cases, false bulkheads, concealed places on board ship, hiding under coals, and so on *ad infinitum,* opium has been found in a sausage skin inside the pigtail of a Chinese, in his boots, anywhere in his clothes or about his person. Drums containing oil would have tins of opium suspended in them, and it would also be found in the packages of all kinds of eatables, Chinese medicines, etc. It has been brought ashore in women's "improvers," in women's clothing, or in their hair. Female smugglers would have their petticoats made with pockets all round, in which the small tins of opium could be put. It can easily be imagined how in the old days of crinolines such a practice could be made use of.

An amusing incident of this kind once occurred. It is usual for the Customs officials to keep a special watch on all vessels arriving from China and the East, and on one occasion when Christie and several other Customs officials were down at a ship's side for this purpose, they observed a very stylishly-dressed young woman go on board the steamer, and afterwards noticed the same person talking very earnestly to a seedy-looking stoker. Their suspicions being naturally aroused, when the woman came ashore Detective Christie accosted her and desired her to get into the cab he had waiting at the wharf. She complied without any apparent hesitation. When the cab was under way, she asked where she was being taken to, and on being informed that she was being conveyed to the Police Watch-house to be examined by the female searcher to see if she had any dutiable goods concealed on her person, she said: "Oh, you need not trouble yourselves about that; I did intend to bring some opium ashore if I could get it, but they had none. You can see for yourself that I have nothing on me," and with that coolly lifted up her garments, showing her underwear, which had been prepared with little pockets round the legs, adding: "You see, I got all ready to bring it, but, as I have none on me, you can't touch me." As her view of the law was correct, there was no alternative but to let her go. Many and many a story could be related of a somewhat similar character, and there is no end to the various methods employed to get this easily-handled article ashore.

Besides the actual smuggling of opium several swindles

in connection with the same drug have also been perpetrated. Two Chinese, named Ah Toon and Ah Low, felt a craving upon them to visit their native land, but, not having sufficient funds for the purpose, cast about for means to get the "needful." They put their heads together to devise some scheme through which by hook or by crook they could raise the wind. The more acute Ah Toon it was who hit upon the idea which was afterwards successfully carried out. It struck him that, as he knew the Chinese merchants in Melbourne were buying up all the opium in the market in anticipation of the prohibition of importation which was subsequently proclaimed, they might be able to fake up a quantity of so-called opium which they could palm off as the real thing. The price the storekeepers were offering for the celebrated Lai Quan brand was much in advance of that paid for ordinary smoking opium. The buyers knew well that in a short time they would realise very high profits. This being so Ah Toon decided that his opium should be nominally of prime quality of the veritable Lai Quan brand. Accordingly Ah Low was set to work to obtain two secondhand cases (in which the drug had been imported) in good preservation with all original shipping marks thereon, showing contents and to buy several tins of the best Lai Quan opium; also to obtain a quantity of empty opium tins of the proper size to fill them with some stuff looking like opium and to label them with fresh labels of the Lai Quan brand.

All this being duly attended to, Ah Toon called upon a well-known Chinese leading storekeeper (who was no favourite by the way with his countrymen), Quong Sing by name, and spun him a pleasant fairy tale, the purport of which was that a German steamer had just arrived from Hong Kong and was now berthed at the lower wharf, that two of the officers, the second and third mates, had brought down in the vessel two cases of the finest Lai Quan opium, which they were prepared to sell and would undertake to smuggle ashore if they could find a buyer. Ah Toon added that if Quong Sing liked to buy he could have it for forty shillings a pound, and of this amount thirty-eight shillings was for the ship's officers and two shillings for himself by way of "cumshaw" or commission. Ah Toon also mentioned that the officers had promised him ten pounds cash for himself if he could find a buyer. Quong immediately accepted the offer on condition that the stuff was veritable Lai Quan, and he was to be satisfied on that point before paying over any money. Ah Toon said the spot where the opium would be landed was very quiet, and that they could go down in a cab and pick up the boxes and bring them to Quong's store, where they could be examined and Quong could satisfy himself as to the contents being genuine. To this Quong agreed, except that as an amendment he would prefer not to bring the boxes straight to his store but to examine them in some other quiet spot.

This was assented to, and Ah Toon went away, ostensibly to go to the steamer, but in reality to his house in Fitzroy to complete the packing of the boxes thus: in each box was placed twelve large tins, each of which contained ten smaller tins, or a total of one hundred and twenty for each case; a small tin of the genuine article was placed inside one of the larger cases and was packed at the end, which was so marked by Ah Toon that he would know which end to open when getting out the tins for Quong's inspection. He had previously arranged with an Austrian and an Englishman to personate two German ship's mates for a tip of five pounds each. One of these could speak broken English only, and the other, to keep up the deception, was to pretend that he did not understand English. A cab was chartered, the two bogus cases picked up, and also the supposititious Germans, and a start made for the spot agreed on with the Chinese buyer. On the way, the party stopped at a second-hand clothing shop and hired two old naval suits, which, on being donned by the men, made them look like a couple of stage pirates.

On arrival at the spot the cases were lifted out of the cab and left in charge of the two make-believe mates. Ah Toon then hurried off for Quong, and on his return with the latter, found the pirates sitting quietly on the boxes waiting for them by the roadside. With much ceremony the two were introduced to Quong, who was apparently much impressed by the uniforms, the faded splendour of which was not apparent in the light of a neighbouring gas lamp, and the boxes were placed in the cab, which, with the whole party, was driven to an hotel in Russell Street. Ah Toon desired that the boxes should be taken inside, but to this the foreign officer objected in broken English, saying the boxes must remain in the cab until they were paid for, and further suggested the boxes be opened in the cab and a few tins taken out for examination in the bar parlour. To this Quong assented, and a hammer and chisel were procured, several tins taken out—these being by the manipulation of Ah Toon those containing the real stuff—and were taken inside the hotel, where the contents were carefully examined by Quong, who pronounced them to be the real thing and of first-class quality. He then took possession of the whole quantity and handed over the price agreed on to Ah Toon, evidently very pleased with his bargain. Ah Toon paid his "Germans" and sent them back with their uniforms.

Quong passed the word round amongst his co-patriots that he had plenty of first-class opium for sale, and soon commenced what promised to be a brisk and profitable trade. Hardly, however, had the first tins disposed of been sampled than his store was beseiged by a crowd of indignant celestials, who declared they had been swindled and vociferously demanded their money back, declaring that Quong was a rogue of the most vermilion type; that all his ancestors had been criminals of the deepest dye; and that virtue had been unknown to his female forebears.

On ascertaining the reason of the outbreak Quong hurriedly examined all the rest of his purchase which he had in stock, and saw at a glance he had been completely "taken down" by Ah Toon. He immediately dashed off to hunt up Ah Toon, and, having run him to earth, after a torrent of invective, declared that unless the former returned the money by noon the next day, he would have a warrant taken out for his arrest. To this Ah Toon, with a bland and childlike smile, replied by informing Quong, as a courteous preliminary, that he was a sanguinary fool. That he, Ah Toon, had never sold any opium to Quong, but that he well knew the latter had smuggled some lately. He further stated that if Quong gave him any trouble, he would inform the Customs authorities of the affair and that Christie would be immediately sent to search his premises and would find the stuff. Also that Quong himself would be arrested and convicted of smuggling, and he playfully reminded Quong that the fine which in that case would be inflicted upon him, would be at least £1,500, and, further, if he were required to pay this, it would increase his total loss on the whole transaction, besides the loss of a reputation which of course, as a virtuous man, the merchant must value more than any amount of money. He also intimated that in order to secure Quong's conviction he, Ah Toon, would himself cheerfully bear witness against him in Court. On the whole, therefore, and as a friend, he would advise Quong to drop the matter, to remember that it was no use to throw good money after bad, and to put up with his first loss. It would always doubtless be a satisfaction, he added, to a good man like Quong to know that his money would be of inestimable benefit to a deserving young man like himself, and enable that estimable individual to see again his native land, and to convey to his aged parents the assurance of his love and affection, and, last but not least, to celebrate those funeral rites to the memory of his ancestors, whom every self-respecting Chinaman held in reverence.

Next day the story of how the unpopular Quong had been taken down by the smart Ah Toon was known all over the Chinese colony in Melbourne. Quong was properly chaffed by his compatriots, and, for a time, any allusion to opium or Ah Toon would elicit sentiments which would never be found in the sayings of Confucius or Mecius. Ah Toon duly departed on the *Tsinan*, but

## OPIUM SMUGGLING.

before his departure he rigged himself out in a stylish European suit of blue serge, Panama hat, patent-leather boots, high collar, brilliant tie, etc., and, with a silver-mounted umbrella on his arm, went to say "Good-bye" to his friends, who received him with all honor.

The following narrative is an instance of an excellently conceived plan to smuggle a considerable quantity of opium, which, however, came to naught through an accident. A syndicate was formed in Melbourne for the purpose of illicitly introducing the drug. The plan was to bring the opium to Melbourne in cases marked "curios," marks and numbers being recorded on the ship's manifest, and on arrival at the Port to nominally transship the goods to another vessel sailing for America. We say "nominally" because it was the intention to substitute bogus cases for the genuine ones whilst the goods were in transit from one ship to another. The plan was not badly conceived, but unfortunately for the speculators they were bowled out in their first attempt. The ship *Aldenham* arrived in Melbourne, having as portion of her cargo four cases which were marked "Curios— James Lloyd, Melbourne consignor John Brown Jr." The cases were duly set out under these marks on the ship's manifest, and were amongst the cargo stowed in the after-hold of the vessel. Though marked "Curios," as a matter of fact, they contained 720 tins of opium, of the value of £2,500. The only person on board the ship who knew what the cases actually contained was Ah Kim, the Chinese chief steward of the *Aldenham*.

The hatchway of the hold in which the boxes were stowed opened into the Chinese boys' quarters, which were under Ah Kim's control, and the latter thought his best plan was to get the boxes up into these quarters and keep them there, instead of letting them go to the sheds with the rest of the cargo. He dared not broach the subject, however, to any of the ship's officers, and thought it best to induce one of the stevedore's labourers working on the cargo to see, when the cases came to hand, that they were put in the place he desired. He accordingly promised £20 to one of these men to do as he wished. The man could not identify the cases, however, in the confusion of discharge of such a large miscellaneous cargo, and being unwilling to lose his twenty pounds he picked out four cases which were like those described by Ah Kim, taking the precaution to lay them with the shipping marks underneath, so that the latter could not be read. He then called Ah Kim and pointed the cases out to him as being the ones he wanted and impressing upon him not to touch them, because the Customs officers were about. Ah Kim was very pleased at having got the cases into his hands, and smilingly paid over the £20.

The Chinaman then covered the cases over with matting and other stuff so that they would not be noticed. The same evening he interviewed one of the Customs night-watchmen, and by means of a heavy bribe induced him to connive at the cases being taken away during the night in a boat which was to come alongside. But during the day Inspector Christie and a posse of officers searched the ship and came across the cases in the boys' quarters. Ah Kim was all innocence, and denied any knowledge of them or that he knew how the boxes got where they were found. The boxes were opened and found to contain ordinary merchandise, to the great astonishment of Ah Kim, who saw at once that the stevedore's man had tricked him, but he dared not say anything, and could only put up with the loss of his £20, though much puzzled as to what had become of the opium.

What had happened in regard to that, however, was this. Strange to say, the same man who had "done" Ah Kim, when working in the hold afterwards came across the real cases and sent them up with other cargo to the Customs shed in the usual course. Whilst handling them his dog-hook had penetrated through the wooden side of one of the cases and also into one of the opium tins, whence oozed out a thin stream of the liquor. A drayman who was carting goods for the Chinese storekeeper for whom the opium was intended, remarking this and smelling the stuff, said to the Customs officer on duty in the shed: "That stuff looks like opium," and the officer thinking it was, promptly seized the goods and took possession of them. The drayman subsequently discovered, to his dismay, that he had been giving away his own employers.

Meanwhile, seeing the game was up as regards the smuggling of the opium straight from the ship by means of the boat, Brown, the European to whom the boxes were addressed and who was in the "swim," not knowing they had been seized by the Customs, had the necessary documents put through, authorising the trans-shipment of four cases of curios from the *Aldenham* to a ship about to leave for the United States. The chagrin of the syndicate may be imagined when, on applying to take delivery of the cases, they were informed of the seizure and found they had suffered such a severe loss. In addition to this, the parties were fined, and, of course, Ah Kim had dropped his £20 also.

## CHAPTER XX.

### BRIDGE AND ITS CONSEQUENCES

IN the course of a detective's career, especially of such a varied nature as was that of Christie, cases occur somewhat different from those with which a detective has usually to deal, and an example of one of these forms the subject of this chapter. A man of position in society, with a young wife and two little children, called on Christie one evening, desiring to have a conversation with him, but requested that the story he was about to narrate might be kept entirely confidential. Christie nodded agreement, and his visitor went on with his story to this effect.

Up to a short time before the interview the husband and wife had been living very happily together. The latter had been everything that could be desired, exemplary in every relation of life. Of late, however, she seemed to have some absorbing interest apart from her household, and was constantly out at her friends' houses, often not returning till late at night. Her manner had become irritable, and her temper very variable. At times she would seem worried and anxious and distrait in her manner. Her domestic affairs no longer seemed to interest her, and the children ceased to occupy her mind and attention. The caller stated that within the last day or so, two occurrences had taken place which had seemed entirely to have upset his wife's nerves, and almost completely prostrated her. Lately a robbery of jewellery belonging to his wife and himself to the value of £300 had been effected from his house. The articles were always kept in an iron deed box in Mrs. ——'s boudoir, the only one key to this box being on a ring with other private keys of the lady. They were never out of her possession, or that of her private companion, an inmate of the house. The whole affair seemed very mysterious, as there had not apparently been any breaking into the house, nor had anything else but the jewellery been taken.

Christie advised his caller to place the matter in the hands of the police detectives for investigation, but Mr. —— said that both his wife and himself were anxious to avoid the inevitable publicity which such a course would entail, and particularly his wife seemed strongly opposed to the suggestion. He had, therefore, called on Christie. "My wife," Mr. —— said, "is in a dreadful state of mind over the affair, and if you can do anything to help us in the matter we should both feel ourselves under an everlasting obligation to you. Come out to my house, and make every enquiry and inspection you may deem necessary, and both my wife and myself will give every possible assistance in unravelling the affair."

To this Christie willingly assented, and, in a very short time called and was introduced to Mrs. ——. The latter, who was an elegantly dressed and attractive looking woman, seemed very nervous and excited, and was evidently unable (or unwilling) to give much information. All that she could say was that she had no suspicions of any one in the house, that her bunch of keys was seldom at any time out of her possession or sight, and the only suggestion she could make was that the robbery had been effected by some one who had used skeleton keys. Christie then carefully looked through the premises, inspected the box, boudoir and general surroundings of the house, and also interviewed each of the other persons attached to the establishment, comprising a coachman and three female servants, besides the lady's companion. As a result, it did not take much penetration to arrive at the conclusion that certainly no burglary had been committed, and further that the theft must have been made by one of the inmates of the house. That being so, the suggestion as to the use of skeleton keys seemed also disposed of, and Christie then again interviewed the lady. "Mrs. ——," said Christie, "it seems to me that the abstraction was made by an inmate of the house. Do you think any one of the servants could have done it by obtaining the use of the key without your knowledge?" To this she replied that the housemaid and her companion were the only persons besides her husband who had access to her rooms. That the housemaid had been with her for five years and enjoyed her fullest trust and confidence, and was in her opinion utterly incapable of such an action; and that her companion had been with her twelve months, and both from her previous life and the knowledge that had been acquired of her character by close association for that time, it hardly seemed likely she could be the culprit, though she added somewhat dubiously, "one never can tell."

Christie took his leave of the lady and accompanied her husband to his study. "Now, sir," he said, "in my opinion there are only three people who were in a position to steal the jewellery, these are your wife, yourself and your wife's companion. You have asked me to take this matter in hand, and I will do so, but I must request you to be good enough to let me conduct it in my own way, giving me all the assistance in your power, and without making any objection to anything I may consider it necessary to do. If you will agree to this I feel sure that in a very short time I shall be able to clear up the mystery, and most probably recover the articles stolen."

Mr. —— readily gave his assurance, and added that he authorised Christie to take any action he might deem requisite, especially in regard to any member of his household or any person connected with it.

Acting therefore with Mr. ——'s concurrence, Christie arranged with the former that he should have an opportunity of meeting the lady's companion, in apparently a casual manner. Accordingly, it was agreed that she should be sent out that evening to post a letter at the pillar box nearby, and that Christie should meet her there apparently accidentally. He was duly strolling on the opposite side of the street opposite the house at eight o'clock, and almost to the minute saw Miss —— come out and walk towards the letter pillar. He then crossed over and met her face to face.

He stopped as if for a minute only to exchange a few courteous remarks, but so contriving that the conversation should continue and become interesting. Each seemed to find the other agreeable, and they were soon strolling in the neighbouring park, where they settled down on a seat secure from observation. Naturally the subject of Christie's recent visit to the house and its exciting cause came up for discussion. The girl did not seem personally disinclined to talk about the robbery, but nothing definite came from her. At last, Christie thought the proper moment had arrived for a flank movement of a decisive character, and changing his manner from that of a polite and interested listener to that of a stern investigator, he said: "Now, Miss ———, from what you have told me of yourself and what I have observed personally, besides what Mrs. ——— has told me, I feel, if you will permit me to say so, though our acquaintance is short, as if I would like to be your friend, and so desire to point out to you in plain terms that you yourself are in a most serious position in regard to this matter of the robbery. Cannot you see that for yourself?" Evidently taken aback by the change in his manner, "What on earth," said the girl in reply, "do you mean, Mr. Christie?" "Am I to understand that I am suspected of having taken the things and the ———s and yourself consider me capable of such an action?"

She was trembling with agitation, the effect of indignation and grief apparently. He continued in reply. "My dear Miss ———, in the course of my long experience in my profession I have often found that persons otherwise blameless in their lives have sometimes, when subjected to a sudden and sharp temptation, given way and committed acts contrary to the whole tenor of their previous lives and foreign to their real natures. A sudden call for means to help some loved one or a great and overwhelming trouble coming unexpectedly has frequently driven people almost out of their senses and caused actions which, committed in a moment, have had far-reaching and serious consequences. You must pardon me if I try to show you exactly in what position you stand in reference to the subject we have been talking over. If my inference is wrong no one will be more pleased than myself to find it so; and if right, I pledge myself to do all I can to extricate you from the difficulty you have got into. Pray, however, calm yourself and try and listen to what I have to say. Indeed, for your own sake and that of your friends and relatives, you should do so, for you are in a position of great peril. You see that everything points to the conclusion that only three people could have had a chance of taking the jewellery, and those three are Mr. and Mrs. —— and yourself."

Here the girl, bursting into tears, interrupted him, "Oh, Mr. Christie, do you really mean that you think I am a thief? I can swear that I have had nothing to do with the robbery, and I know as little as yourself who did it. Indeed, I am perfectly innocent of any complicity in the theft. I cannot bear being under the faintest suspicion in regard to it. The disgrace of being accused merely will kill me or I shall kill myself. Oh, Mr. Christie, I cannot, cannot, believe that the world can be so cruel. I am trying to keep calm, I know I must do so in order to clear myself of this terrible suspicion, if in God's mercy I can ever be clear of it. Before God, I assert my innocence and beg you to believe me and help me to prove it."

Christie, who had been observing her intently, here replied, "Well, Miss ——, I have before told you that even if you were the culprit, I would do my best to help you out of the scrape and if you were not, still more I would endeavour, to the best of my ability, to establish the lack of complicity on your part in this affair. Now, I am inclined to believe your statement that you had nothing to do with it, but you must see that if I do so we are driven to the conclusion that it was one of the owners themselves, and that one, for obvious reasons, must be Mrs. —— herself. My dear girl, pull yourself together, and let us see what we can do. I notice you have a very intelligent mind, and, if you can only think clearly, must be able to help me greatly. Certainly, the idea of ascribing the abstraction to Mrs. —— herself seems somewhat wild on the face of it. It is hardly credible, that a woman like her living in ease and comfort with her husband, whom she loves, and who loves her, and her children, having ample means apparently at her disposal, should commit an act of this kind without any adequate motive. Mr. ——," he continued, "has already told me he was always ready to supply his wife's pecuniary needs without question. Now think, is there, or was there, any possible reason for her wishing to raise money? Was she in any pecuniary difficulty of which she would not like to tell her husband, for instance? I have known of women being subject to blackmail and driven to resort to all kinds of means to satisfy the demands made on them. Was there anything of the kind in this case? Now, I see you are not yet quite yourself. Remain here for a few minutes, and whilst I am away try and reflect quietly over the situation. You will find it your best policy to treat me as a friend and give me your entire confidence. You must remember the great point is to clear yourself, and that the consequences to Mrs. ——, if she were indeed the person responsible for the abstraction, can be nothing like those to yourself even if nothing more than a suspicion attaches to you. I will be back in five minutes.

Now try and look at the matter from a common sense point of view. I pledge you my word anything you will tell me shall be kept strictly secret, and further, what I am sure will have great weight with you that so far as Mrs. —— is concerned, even if she committed the deed, the worst that could happen to her would be a scene with her husband, who we both know is of a generous and forgiving disposition, and would not be hard upon her. No one else need know anything of it."

So saying, he left her sitting with her handkerchief to her face, evidently crying.

When Christie later returned to her, he found her comparatively calm and collected. "Well, Mr. Christie," she said, "I find myself in some difficulty of conscience. Mrs. —— and, indeed, the whole family, have been most kind to me during my twelve months' stay with them. My salary has been liberal and Mrs. —— has always treated me more as a friend than a paid companion and has, to a certain extent, given me her confidence. I owe a great deal both to her and Mr. ——, and I feel it would be a disloyal act for me to betray that confidence, and I cannot make up my mind to do so. I see the alternative, but bitter as it would be, I cannot act otherwise. God knows what this determination will cost me, but I feel it to be the right one."

Christie was much taken aback at these words. He had thought that the girl, terrified at the implied accusation against herself, would, on reflection, have been willing to have done anything and told anything to escape the suspicion raised against her. He had not expected, however, to find such firmness of character in a young woman placed in such a trying position. He could see from her manner that, if the girl would only speak out, he would probably obtain at once a clue to the whole business, but he also saw that the way to induce her to do so would not be by veiled threats, cajolery, or prospect of reward. She was of too honorable a nature as well as of too firm a character to be influenced by considerations of this kind, and it could only be by influencing her better judgment or commanding her reason that he could hope to succeed with her. So he had deliberately to match his brain against hers and endeavour to make her see wherein the path of true loyalty to her employer lay, and to this end to set before her in plain words what he conceived to be her real duty. This he proceeded to do. He admitted she owed much to her employers, and that she should be loyal to them above all. But after all, in what did true loyalty consist? He observed that he felt convinced that Miss —— was aware of something which would implicate Mrs. ——. What the girl had to consider was what would be of most benefit to the greatest number. If she remained silent, the greatest possible harm to every one concerned might ensue. If Mrs. —— had taken the articles, it must have been only to sell them to obtain money. That fact was bound to become known sooner or later, and the result might be a permanent breaking up of a happy home, and disruption between husband and wife. Suspicion against the latter would inevitably arise in her husband's mind, leading possibly to her separation from him and her children, and this and more would be upon her head as the consequences of her obstinate silence. On the other hand, he again reiterated that for her to speak would be productive of benefit only. The mystery would be cleared up, the jewellery restored, confidence between husband and wife re-established, and the latter would have a warning which would beneficially affect her whole future life. In the interests of others, he urged her to give way. After a few minutes consideration in silence, Miss —— turned to him saying, "I must confess that what you have said has almost entirely removed my scruples, though I still feel some hesitation in complying with your request. Still, I will now tell you all I know, on the understanding that you will never divulge my name as the source of your information unless with my consent."

She then proceeded to inform him that within the last few months Mrs. —— had become very intimate with three other ladies whose names she mentioned, and that the four frequently met at each other's houses. Mrs. ——'s particular friend was a Mrs. ——, who lived in a neighbouring suburb and at whose house she had spent a great deal of time. This lady was an inveterate bridge player, as indeed were all three of Mrs. ——'s friends, and had induced her employer to make a constant fourth at their games, with the result that Mrs. —— had acquired a strong taste for the game and had become a slave to the vice of gambling, though entirely unknown to her husband. Unfortunately, however, for the lady, the other players were much more adept at the game than herself and she had lost (for her) large sums of money to them which she was unable to pay. These other women had lately been dunning her for the money, and she had latterly become much worried over the fact of the sums she owed to them. She dared

## BRIDGE AND ITS CONSEQUENCES.

not let her husband know of her difficulties, and she had become very despondent and unhappy and at her wits' end. Miss —— did not suggest any connection between the two facts of the loss of the jewellery and these debts, but after the detective's remarks evidently now thought there was some connection between the two. Christie proceeded to question Miss —— further. He asked her whether her employer ever wrote to any of the persons whose names she had mentioned, to which she replied that she frequently did so, especially to Mrs. ——, the organiser of the card parties. The notes were posted in the letter pillar near which Christie had met her. Christie then requested her that on the next occasion she had to post one of these notes, she would pretend to do so, but keep it and hand it to Mr. —— without his wife's knowledge. This she undertook to do. He further desired her when next Mrs. —— was going to town, to let him know by telephone, supplying her with the number with which she was to communicate. The message was to be for a "Captain Mitchell," and to say, "The lady will be sailing at about . . . .," giving the probable time of Mrs. —— leaving by the tram.

Next day he communicated with the husband, desiring him to take any letter handed to him by Miss —— and peruse it.

The following morning Christie received a telephonic message saying the lady was leaving at eleven o'clock. He then posted himself on Princes Bridge to watch the incoming tram cars, and in about half an hour saw a car stopping on the bridge at the Flinders Street crossing, on the dummy of which Mrs. —— was seated. He jumped upon the back of the car, and when the latter reached Collins Street saw Mrs. —— change to another car going up the street into which he also got, without being observed. The car stopped opposite a pile of buildings where Mrs. —— got out and remained a little while looking into a shop window. Presently a man came up to her and, after a few minutes' conversation, Christie observed the lady hand him a small parcel, which she had taken out of her peggy bag. The two then proceeded inside the building to the place of business of the man, whom Christie had recognised as a dealer in jewellery, etc., and a kind of money lender. She remained there about ten minutes, then came out and went into a fashionable draper's shop in the vicinity. After that she took the tram, evidently on her way home. The matter was now clear. The wife had taken the jewellery and pawned or sold it to the dealer to raise money to pay her gambling debts. The companion was innocent.

Christie considered that it would be advisable to take the husband entirely into his confidence, and leave it to him to decide what further (if anything) should be done in the matter. Accordingly, he telephoned to Mr. —— to call and see him at his office before leaving for home in the afternoon, and the latter did so. "I presume," said Mr. ——, "you have something to tell me about the jewellery?"

"Yes," replied Christie, "I know who took it, and where to find it."

"That is good news, indeed, but tell me all about it."

"Before doing so," said Christie, "I must tell you that I fear the information I have to give you will be very painful to you, and give you a great shock. I shall decline to reveal anything unless you will give me your word of honor that if I do you will be magnanimous and forgiving to the guilty. That you will remember that we all have our evil hours when temptation is too strong for us and we sometimes succumb. In other words, that you will show mercy, and pardon a weakness which perhaps you cannot understand, but which nevertheless is the only reason of the fault."

Mr. —— changed color, and exhibited considerable alarm.

"Tell me quickly who it was? I promise you all you ask. I will forgive the fault."

"Well, then, it was your wife," said Christie.

"Good God, man," said ——, "you are dreaming. You might as well say I did it myself. She is incapable of doing such a thing. It is an insult to imagine and a double insult to give expression to such an idea. I have always given her all she wanted in the way of money, and your suggestion is unthinkable. I have always heard that you detectives make up your minds beforehand, and then devote all your energies in proving the case against the person decided upon in your own minds. You have jumped to a conclusion in this instance, and are wrong. Miss ——'s bright eyes have been too much for you, experienced as you are, and she has twisted you round her finger. If this is all you can do I regret I ever came to you, and will not trouble you any further. Good day."

Christie, while listening, felt his anger rising, but keeping himself in check, tried to make allowance for the speaker, knowing what a blow he had dealt him.

"Wait," he said, and "listen quietly. My first impulse, on hearing what you have just said was to tell you you might go, and go a good long way, too. But I know you to be a reasonable man and feel convinced that when you have heard all I have to narrate, you will change your opinion."

He then proceeded to recount all that is related above, and as he spoke, the distress in Mr. ——'s face seemed to deepen. When Christie had concluded his narration, his listener looked ten years older. For a time his lips trembled, and he was evidently overcome with emotion. "My wife," he murmured, "my dear Emily to do a thing like this! Even now I cannot believe it."

"Mr. ——," said Christie, "remember what I said just now. You must not condemn for one fault. Your wife has got under the influence of a lot of society harpies who have taken advantage of her, got her in their power and been bleeding her. Your anger should be directed against them, not your wife, who is young and inexperienced. It is those bridge-playing women who have done the mischief, and if we could, I should like to make them suffer for it. But I fear we cannot get at them. Now, if you want this matter completely settled up, there are other things to be done. Shall we go on with them?"

Mr. —— reflected a little, and then said, "Certainly, it must be followed up to the bitter end now."

"Very well then, when you get home, say nothing to your wife of what I have told you; let your manner be as usual or more affectionate even. Whilst at dinner take an opportunity of remarking casually that she looks out of sorts and that you hope she is not taking the loss of the jewellery to heart. Also, ask her if she went into town to-day."

Mr. ——, on his return home, did as Christie suggested, and in answer to his enquiries was informed by his wife that she felt very much upset by the loss, and that she had started to go to town that day, but felt so unwell when she arrived at the tram that she had returned without doing so. Of course, a falsehood.

Mr. —— called on Christie the next morning, and, after telling him what had passed between his wife and himself, produced a letter which had been handed to him by Miss ——, and which she had received from Mrs. —— to post the evening before. He now desired Christie to peruse it. It was addressed to Mrs. ——, the promoter of the bridge parties, and read as follows:—

"I will be up on Wednesday evening, as I am 'flush of coin,' as they say in sporting parlance.
"E."

At Christie's suggestion this letter was resealed, and was duly posted on the way to the dealer's, whither they now proceeded for the purpose of recovering the articles.

They introduced themselves to the man, but when they spoke of a robbery, he denied all knowledge of any such transaction. Christie, however, insinuated that they were by no means accusing him as acting as a "fence" or receiver of stolen property, but thought it was quite possible that he had been induced to lend money in the ordinary way of business on some articles, believing they were the property of the person offering them. The man then immediately fell into the snare and said, "Oh, now you are talking sense. I did lend some money to a lady on her jewellery, which she brought to me, a straight and *bona fide* transaction which I have no reason to conceal, seeing it was her own property."

They then asked the man to show it to them Christie pretended to inspect it critically, and then suddenly said, "Why, a portion of this is a man's jewellery. You said it was a woman's, and her own property," and turning to Mr. ——, asked him if he identified the articles, which the latter unhesitatingly did.

The man, who looked confused, here broke in, saying that the lady who had brought the things, had stated that as regards these particular articles, they had belonged to her husband, who was dead. The man added, "If you will give me the £100 I lent on it, you may have them. I will forego all profit."

"Not so fast," said Christie, "the man's things were stolen and are now in your possession, which requires explanation. I cannot advise Mr. —— to return the money, but urge him to apply to the detectives with a view to prosecution. You are certainly criminally liable and deserve to lose over this transaction, which you must have known was a very fishy one at best. We can make no bargain with you, but if Mr. —— is inclined to be generous, he might give you half what you say you advanced."

To this the man, after some hesitation, assented, as he said he did not want to be shown up in the Police Court; the money was paid by cheque, and they left, taking the jewellery with them.

"Now," said Christie, "as to-morrow is Sunday, can you tell me if your wife is likely to be out?"

"Yes," said Mr. ——, "a lady friend is going to call for her in the morning in a motor-car to take her to Sandringham, where they will spend the day and not return till late in the afternoon."

"Then," said Christie, "I will call at your house immediately at noon for the purpose of trying to locate the money, which ought to be in your possession, and before those bloodsuckers get hold of it."

Mr. —— assented, and Christie duly called at the time mentioned. With Mr. ——'s consent Miss ——'s assistance was invoked in order to restore the various drawers and receptacles in the boudoir to their former orderly condition after search; he himself remaining in the study. After a prolonged turning over, nothing of interest was found until in taking out the lower drawer of the wardrobe a lot of letters in the bottom came to light, and in the cavity between the drawer and outside skin of the wardrobe was a paper scent box which, in handling, Christie knew from its weight contained gold. Taking both box and letters down to Mr. —— in his study, they were duly examined by the two. The letters were from the bridge friends relating to past debts, and asking for money and the box contained £60 in gold. The letters were replaced, as also the box minus its contents, which Mr. —— retained. It was then arranged that the wife should be kept in entire ignorance for the present, awaiting further developments.

On the Wednesday evening Mrs. —— dressed ready to go to the bridge party, and then evidently with a view to get the money, unknown to Miss ——, who was assisting in her toilet, sent the latter out on some trivial errand. On the latter's return what was her dismay to find her employer lying apparently lifeless on the floor, with the drawer of the wardrobe open. Evidently, on finding the gold gone, she had fainted. The companion applied restoratives, and then called the husband, who came at once. When his wife regained consciousness or partially so, she exclaimed, "I had a box of sovereigns in that drawer, and someone has stolen it." To this her husband replied that she was talking nonsense, but something had been going on which must come to an end, and commanded her, as soon as she was fit to do so, to come down to his study where he had something to say to her.

His wife was much impressed by the gravity of his manner. She was, however, quite unprepared for what met her eye when, shortly afterwards, she appeared in her husband's study for when she did so, she saw displayed on the table, not only the gold which she had hidden in her wardrobe, and subsequently missed, but every article of the jewellery she had deposited with the dealer.

Quite overcome at the sight, she sank into a chair unable at first to speak, and could only gaze at her husband with imploring looks as if begging for lenient treatment, and wondering what he intended to do. Too late, the consequences of her folly had come home to her. She felt without excuse, and when brought face to face with the evidence of her error, began to realise what she had done and the full extent to which she had imperilled her future happiness and that of those connected with her. Seeing her terrible distress, Mr. —— felt that if he followed his own inclination, he would without saying more at once relieve her of all anxiety. Still, in her own interest, for her own sake, he knew that this was an occasion which should be utilised to make a lasting impression upon her mind, and one which might have permanent effect upon her, and influence her future life.

"Now, Emily," he said, "I can see that you understand that I am aware of what you have done. I do not wish to overwhelm you with reproaches or increase the distress which you obviously feel at the present moment, but it will be absolutely necessary before we can be restored to anything like the former terms of affection and confidence in which we lived, that you tell me everything which has induced you to act in this terrible manner, and above all, that you will give me your solemn undertaking that in future you will never, under any possible circumstances, play cards for money, or have any concealments from me. Further, you must also promise to cease to have any association with these women, who, I am convinced, have led you into mischief, and been the main cause of your troubles."

His wife then related the steps which had led up to the catastrophe. How, at first, she had been induced, when spending the evening at Mrs. ———'s, to join in a game of bridge for small stakes, and won a little. How, by degrees, the desire had grown upon her, and the excitement of play became her main interest. How her so-called friends had laughed at her scruples, and put her up to the little tricks they each had resorted to, to deceive their husbands in order to obtain the money for the game. Gradually she was drawn in, till she found herself fearfully involved. The sums she could retain out of her housekeeping money or obtain under various pretexts from her husband for special purposes all went to pay losses at cards. The women, however, encouraged her by saying if she kept on she would soon retrieve her fortunes, and in the hope of doing so and winning enough to pay all she owed to the various members of the circle, she kept on and on with the result that she found herself without money, and heavily in debt to them. Then they began to press her for payment. Hitherto, they had told her it did not matter, and they would wait, but once entirely in their clutches they seemed to be desirous of making an end of their victim. The principle sum was owing to Mrs. ——, one of those women, who, scheming and unprincipled in reality, yet to the world appeared merely a good-natured person who liked to see her friends enjoying themselves. As a matter of fact, her establishment was kept up largely by her gains at cards, at which she was most expert. She was, moreover, when she chose, most winning and attractive in her manner, and could greatly influence many who were brought into contact with her, generally however, to their disadvantage. Many men could tell a tale of devices by which they had willingly or otherwise been cajoled out of sums of money, some of them considerable. She made bets which she never paid when she lost, yet when she won exacted in the most seductive way the utmost return. Without passion, and heartless, yet she could simulate the woman of repressed feelings, of strong physical desires, and of tender affection, never going over the border line, yet as near it as possible without doing so. Many men fell victims to her rapacity. She had the face of a madonna, but the soul of a sexless being, intent only on her own gratification. No wonder such a woman could ensnare an innocent young woman like Mrs. ——, and by imperceptible stages lead her on to her destruction.

Mr. —— knew much of this lady by repute, and could readily believe all that his wife told him regarding her, and easily understand the full force of the influence exercised by her. His wife then went on to say how after days and nights of torment she had taken the desperate course already related. In tears she confessed her fault, and begged her husband's forgiveness. She promised by all she held most sacred, she would entirely abandon her acquaintance with this gambling set, and that she would never, in the rest of her life, play cards for money. She said she had known no real happiness since she had commenced gambling. It was only in the excitement of play she could forget. Her days were wearisome, her nights a terror. She had ultimately got into such a state of mind that she was not responsible for her actions. The sneers of her "friends" at her delay in payments, the fear they might apply to her husband, the depth of whose affection and whose kindness of heart were not then understood by her, terrified her beyond endurance. It was some hint from Mrs. —— that led her to think of raising money on the jewellery. With specious argument she pointed out that as it was really Mrs. ——'s property, the latter had a right to do as she liked with it; that hundreds of women in society from peeresses downwards raised loans upon their valuables without their husbands' knowledge and that it was an ordinary and perfectly innocent proceeding which there could be no hesitation in adopting.

Influenced by these arguments the step was taken, and, as regards her husband's property, as he never used it, or very rarely, she thought she would be safe in taking that too, as she hoped the loan would be for a short time, and she might, with good fortune, be able to redeem it very quickly before the abstraction was known. Unfortunately for her, her husband had asked for a pair of sleeve links which was in the box, and hence she had to invent the tale of the robbery to account for their loss.

"My dear," said Mr. ——, " I see how this all came about. I do not wish to preach or work on your feelings by pointing out the full extent of your error. I fully and unreservedly forgive you your fault, and accept your assurance for the future. We must, however, settle this matter up once and for all, and then we will never refer to it again. The first thing is to deal with those women who have been fleecing you. There must, however, be no scandal or talk; the thing must be managed quietly. You shall not go to any of their houses again, but send each of them a note telling them to call and see you next Monday at 4 p.m., saying you will then pay each the money you owe them, which I will give you for the purpose."

This was accordingly done, but had no effect, as the ladies scented trouble. It was as well, perhaps, that they did not come, as Mr. —— intended to be present, and his remarks might have been more forcible than polite. Crossed cheques to each were accordingly sent, thus enabling payment to be traced, and as these were signed by Mr. ——, it would be brought home to the recipients that he was aware of their "little games."

They had known nothing of the jewellery episode, and would probably conclude that Mrs. —— had cajoled her husband into paying the money. Anyway, no cheque was returned.

Christie was warmly thanked by Mr. —— for his part in the affair, and on Miss ——'s next birthday, she received from her employers a handsome bracelet. She is still a valued inmate of the house, though it is thought that the frequent visits of a good-looking young stockbroker to the villa, are not altogether owing to his friendship for the owners.

## CHAPTER XXI.

### STORY OF A DIAMOND NECKLACE.

AT the time this incident occurred, Sydney was a free-trade port, whilst very heavy duties were levied on most importations coming into Victoria. One of the heaviest was that on jewellery, and this duty very considerably enhanced the cost to purchasers. Seeing that on purchases made in New South Wales no such charge had been levied, it is evident that people if they had the opportunity would buy in that State in preference to Victoria. Jewellery is so valuable, and carried in such small parcels that it was an article which was being perpetually smuggled over, concealed on the persons of travellers. It became a regular thing with some people who could afford it to go over to Sydney and make their purchases there. This practice, of course, occasioned considerable loss to Victorian tradesmen, and many and loud were the complaints made as to the surreptitious introduction of goods from New South Wales. The Customs officials used every device to check the practice, but without personal search, which was impossible, it is clear that valuable articles which could be carried on the person, could easily be overlooked. Of course, when the officers had reliable information a search of the person of the suspected individual was made, but such cases were very few and a great number escaped.

In these days of Federation, one can hardly understand how the people of Australia could have put up with the inconvenience of the examination of luggage on the border between the different States. Absurd and irritating cases were always occurring, which often provoked a great deal of ridicule or ill-feeling. In cases where there were two towns, such as Wodonga in Victoria, and Albury, in New South Wales, almost touching each other, the boundary between being an imaginary line only, this was especially the case. The boundary had to be patrolled constantly, every bridge had to have gates and a watch-house for the Customs officer on it, and every traveller crossing had to be examined and any packages he had with him inspected. The local tradesmen in the Victorian township who had to pay duty on the goods they vended would see their customers going over the bridge to the township at the end to make purchases in New South Wales. On the clothing actually in wearing, or on second-hand clothing, carried in his luggage, the Customs could not legally charge duty, and so it was not an uncommon sight to see a Victorian resident stroll across to the other side, and afterwards return, in all the gorgeousness of new apparel which he had purchased there free of duty.

Owing to the outcry of the local shopkeepers the Customs officers were especially vigilant, and carried out their work in some cases with a minuteness which it must be confessed was at times ludicrous as well as annoying to the victim. Thus, on one occasion a shearer coming from New South Wales was bailed up and his swag inspected. Inside was found a shirt. Then a great argument arose as to whether the shirt had been worn or not. Its owner asserted that it had, whilst the officer insisted to the contrary, basing his assertions on the fresh appearance of the garment. A vast amount of talk on the spot and the correspondence with the head office ensued, and, at last, the owner was given the benefit of the doubt, and got his shirt duty free, escaping payment of about 1/6 duty, and also prosecution as a daring smuggler. On another occasion, another man had bought a pair of boots which he had in his swag and had not worn. On being stuck up for the duty, a heated controversy arose between him and the official, which ended in the owner leaving the boots in the hands of the officer, with the remark that the Customs might keep "the —— boots." They were subsequently sent in the usual course to Melbourne, where, owing to their enormous size, tradition avers, they were ultimately used as coal scuttles.

Now, during the time this state of things existed, a wealthy merchant of Melbourne visited Sydney, and whilst there called in at a jeweller's shop where there was a diamond necklace which had been seen and coveted by the merchant's spouse on a recent visit to the city. The merchant, anxious to please his wife, purchased the jewellery for £800, tendering a cheque for the amount, drawn on a Melbourne bank. The jeweller, as he did not know the drawer of the cheque personally, and as it was on a Melbourne bank, intimated that before handing over the necklace, he must either have the cash or the cheque endorsed by some leading resident of Sydney, known to himself. The merchant enquired if the endorsement of the proprietor of the well-known hotel, where he was staying, would be sufficient, and receiving an answer in the affirmative, immediately returned thither and found the proprietor in the bar parlour. He told him what had taken place, saying that as he had to leave next day and did not want to disappoint his wife, who wished to wear the necklace at a forthcoming Mayor's Ball, he would be obliged if the landlord would endorse the cheque, which the latter willingly did, and offered to place the jewels in his safe till the next morning.

"Oh," said the purchaser, "I will put the necklace on, under my shirt over my singlet, so that I can not only carry it safely but also dodge the Customs. The landlord jokingly warned him that he had better look out for Christie, if he was going to play that game.

"Oh, I'm not afraid of Christie," he answered, "because he is a good old friend of mine, and would not suspect me." He then returned to the shop, got the necklace and duly left next day by steamer *via* Hobart for Melbourne, with the jewellery concealed as he intended.

So far so good. But it so happened that in the bar parlor was sitting in an obscure corner, a man to all appearance drunk or asleep, who heard all that was said between the two. This man had himself been previously detected in smuggling in Melbourne and had been convicted and fined; being a poor man, he was quite ruined and reduced to the last extremity and was completely on his beam-ends. This man also knew the name of the purchaser of the necklace. The Victorian law allowed to informers a third of the sum netted by the Department in cases of conviction for smuggling, and it occurred to this man that here was an opportunity to improve his financial position. He accordingly at once wrote to Christie giving him a full account of what he had heard, and wound up by saying he was "damned" hard up, and would be glad to have the reward,

The detective met the steamer and duly interviewed the passenger, who produced the necklace from the place where he had it concealed, and handed it over. At the Customs House next morning, having elected to be dealt with by the Minister instead of being prosecuted in Court, he was fined a total sum of £616, which he promptly paid.

All his troubles, however, were not ended yet. The Melbourne Harbor Trust levy a wharfage rate on all packages coming by sea, and, at that time, the Customs collected these rates for the Trust as their agents. The merchant was informed before the necklace could be handed to him, that he must pay twopence wharfage rate upon it. Although having parted with such a large sum of money, he seemed much exasperated by this demand, and said; "I'll be damned if I pay another penny," but on finding that he would not get the necklace without paying the trifle demanded, he threw down a three-penny-bit, saying that the Department could "keep the change." His manner was so offensive to the Collector that he was informed that the correct sum must be tendered as the cashier was not required to give change. With that he went away and came back with the necessary twopence, remarking that the other penny would do to buy a *Herald* with, and added "fortunately this affair will not get into the paper as it was dealt with by the Department."

What was his disgust and annoyance when, on purchasing a paper as he left the Customs House, he found a report headed—"The Merchant and His Diamonds"— "Great Bowl Out," and read a detailed account of his trouble in its columns. In a towering rage, he rushed back to the office, and fiercely demanded of Christie whether he had given the information to the paper. The latter stated he had not. It may here be remarked in conclusion that it was not the policy of the Department to avoid publicity in such cases, the object of inflicting fines was as much to warn others against smuggling as to punish the actual offender, and consequently a full account of such instances was always given to the daily press. Since Federation the department adopts the better system of prosecuting in the Court, when any wilful evasion of the law is suspected or known.

## CHAPTER XXII.
## MISCELLANEOUS CUSTOMS FRAUDS.

### MARRIAGE PRESENTS.

A WELL-KNOWN Melbourne man was about to be married to the daughter of a wealthy squatter residing in a fashionable suburb of that city. So far so good; but, when the Customs detective was travelling to New South Wales a day or so before the wedding, he engaged in conversation with a fellow passenger. The conversation turned to smuggling, and the passenger, referring to the marriage, narrated how the bridegroom-elect had been to Sydney, where he had bought some valuable wedding presents, and had smuggled these into Victoria. On hearing this, Christie got out at Seymour and took train back to Melbourne. On enquiry he found that the "smuggler" had just gone off to be married.

The detective then drove off to the bride's residence, where he found a large assembly of the rank and fashion of Melbourne; marquees on the lawn, and everything indicating a function of the most elaborate kind. He sent in his card to the bridegroom who, however, returned a message by the footman to say that he was too much engaged at that time to see the detective. Christie then sent for the master of the house. The latter came out and smiling said, "There is nothing here in your line, Mr. Christie. My daughter is to be married this afternoon, but come in and tell me your business.' He then took

Detective-Inspector J. M. Christie.

Christie into the dining-room, where a bottle of champagne was opened and duly discussed. The detective then informed his host what his business was. The prospective father-in-law was much taken aback at the revelation, and, on the jewellery having been described to him, informed the detective that it had all been distributed in presents to the bride and the bridesmaids. He then went and fetched the smuggler, who, after fencing a little, finally owned up to everything. The detective, with the sanction of the authorities, who did not wish to cause a large number of innocent people to suffer for the fault of one, accepted the guarantee of the squatter that the jewellery should be duly produced by the offender at the Customs House the next day. The culprit was promptly fined £200, and required to pay the full duty on the articles.

## A TALE OF A PIG.

The *Loch Vannacher* was at one time a well-known trader to Melbourne, in charge of Captain Bennett, who was popular with all who knew him. In 1899 the vessel arrived, and was duly berthed at the Victoria Dock. The ship had on board two small well-bred Berkshire pigs, which animals much took the fancy of the proprietor of one of the Melbourne hotels, who had a farm in the country and who became very anxious to secure one of these animals for breeding purposes. The quarantine laws of Victoria are very strict as regards animals, especially swine, and the introduction of any such animal involved long delay in quarantine, and many other rather vexatious though necessary formalities, besides considerable expense. In order, therefore, to avoid all this trouble and cost, it was determined to try and outwit the Customs, and land the pig surreptitiously. To that end the hotelkeeper's wife was taken into the plot, and it was arranged that the pig was to be brought ashore, having been previously dressed up as a baby in long clothes, with hood and covering over the head and carried in the lady's arms as an infant.

All went well up to a certain point, and the day chosen for the attempt being Sunday, not many people were about. Now Bennett had a parrot which, amongst other things, had been taught to say, "Look out, here's Christie," and, strange to say, just as the lady reached the gangway, and was going down the ladder to the wharf, the bird commenced to yell out these words. Probably startled by the bird, the lady slipped and her stumble so alarmed the "infant" she was carrying, that it squealed in a manner to raise the whole neighbourhood. A Customs watchman came running up, attracted by the squeals, and on seeing him coming, the would-be smugglers took the "baby" hurriedly back on board the ship, divested it of its finery and replaced it in its stye, where it was no doubt much happier than in the lady's arms.

This story came to the ears of the authorities, and Christie was instructed to make enquiries with a view to gaining sufficient information for a prosecution which would, if successful, have involved the parties in double penalties, seeing that both customs and quarantine laws would have been broken had the attempt been carried out successfully. As, however, the act had not been actually committed, though the intention was clear enough, nothing could be done and the matter was dropped.

## BOGUS VALUE.

In one instance, in regard to the under-valuation of goods, the Department was cleverly "put in the soup" by a sharp importer. There is a provision in the Customs Act under which the Department has the power, when there is a reason to suppose goods have been under-valued for duty (and failing more severe measures), to take over the goods at the importer's valuation for duty with 10 per cent. added. Thus, if the importer represented the value of his importation to be, say £100, the Department, by paying him £110, could acquire the ownership of the goods and sell them. Usually, when such a course was adopted, the Department made a considerable profit on the transaction.

In the case to be recorded, certain goods were imported about which the suspicion of the officers was aroused by sundry hints from outside quarters. From the information conveyed to them there seemed every reason to suppose the value of the goods had been much understated, and that it would be a safe thing to make use of the power the law gave them in the case. Accordingly the goods were duly taken over, and the importer paid for them. When, however, the sale took place the result was most disappointing, and a considerable loss was incurred, much to the chagrin of the officers. Enquiry at the bank had elicited the fact that the importer had obtained advances upon his bills of lading which indicated the same values as the importer had declared to at the Customs House, and this fact seemed to show the importer's estimate of the proper value was correct. It afterwards appeared, however, that the whole affair was a "put-up job." The goods were not really worth anything like the value attached to them by the importer, and consequently both the Department and the bank had "fallen in." The former in paying more than the goods were worth, and the latter in advancing more money than their value justified.

This fiasco, however, made the officials very careful in subsequent cases of the same kind, and in future the power was only exercised when a good profit would accrue to the Treasury from the transaction.

## A DETECTIVE PARSON.

On one occasion in 1894 one of the passengers travelling in the overland express from Sydney to Melbourne was a tall, somewhat severe-looking High Church Anglican minister, who took his seat in the train at Albury and forthwith became absorbed apparently in a Church paper. At Albury, prior to Federation, the Victorian Customs' officials overhauled the luggage, and made enquiry of the passengers from New South Wales, as to whether they had any dutiable goods in their possession. Amongst the passengers in the carriage in which the reverend gentleman had taken his seat, there was an elegantly-dressed woman. The word went round that the Customs' officers were coming, and that passengers should have bags, etc., ready for inspection.

If any one, just at this time, had been looking at the reverend traveller, the observer would have noticed that, though apparently engrossed in reading his paper, he was gazing over the top of it into the mirror fixed above the opposite seat, and that what he saw there appeared to interest him exceedingly. What the reverend gentleman was looking at was this:—The lady, on hearing the officers were coming, immediately took some parcels out of her bag and pushed them down the seat behind her, but in such a manner as would not be observed by the person alongside, though she had evidently forgotten the mirror opposite, in which the parson was, however, able to observe all her actions.

When the Customs officers had passed and the lady had told him she had nothing dutiable, the clergyman turned to his neighbour saying, "Madame, I regret to trouble you, but you have just informed the Customs' officers you have no dutiable goods in your possession. May I ask what those parcels were that you have just pushed down behind you?"

The lady was covered with confusion, but, relying apparently upon the clerical character of her questioner, tried to "bluff him off," but seeing this, the apparent parson altered his tune, and to her astonishment and that of all the other passengers in the car, and to the great amusement of all but the lady herself, told her he was Inspector Christie of the Customs. She then confessed herself a would-be smuggler, and surrendered the articles, with the usual result.

## CHAPTER XXIII.

### "A CLOUD OF WITNESSES."

IN 1890 a number of 'cute Yankees formed themselves into a company for the purpose of publishing and selling in Australia a large lithograph picture called "A Cloud of Witnesses." The picture was to commemorate the opening of the Melbourne Exhibition, and was to contain three hundred likenesses of the best-known citizens, and most prominent men in the community, with the Governor (Lord Loch) and the Judges in the centre. It was anticipated that each person whose likeness was included, would subscribe for one or more of these pictures. To subscribers, the price of the first copy was to be ten guineas, and for subsequent copies five guineas. Prior to publication, canvassers were employed to go round inviting subscriptions, the canvassers being supposed to obtain a printed order. Many orders were sent in; one canvasser being apparently very successful, as he obtained three times as many orders as all the rest of the canvassers put together, most of the orders he sent in being for one picture and five copies, the prices of which would total £36 15s. These orders were all apparently properly signed by the person presumably giving the order.

The picture was produced in America, and was what is known as a "photogravure." On importation into Melbourne the consignment was duly passed through the Customs, and the value of each copy declared to be two shillings only. Soon after the arrival of the photos..

the canvasser called upon several of the principal officials of the Department and informed them that the picture was now available for distribution, and that he had brought the six which each of them had ordered. These officials declared that they had never given any such order, though they remembered having signed a paper which purported to be a kind of general approval of the idea, and which document was also signed by a considerable number of other well-known persons; and that the person who had procured their names to this paper had given them distinctly to understand that the signatures were only intended to show the Company that people were interested in the work it intended to bring out and that no pecuniary liability was implied in the fact of their signing, nor was any such liability expressed in the wording of the document to which they had put their names. The officers, however, were shown printed orders bearing their usual signatures for the pictures and copies, and they could not deny that these signatures had all the appearances of being genuine, though they were certain they had never given any such orders, and could not understand how the signatures came to be attached to them. It was manifestly absurd to suppose that whatever one or two from vanity or recklessness might possibly have done, a number of ordinarily careful men with limited incomes would have each made himself liable for such an amount for a mere picture. The canvasser, however, insisted on leaving the pictures, saying as they had been ordered they would have to be paid for, but as he was departing the pictures were gathered up and pitched downstairs after him. Proceedings at law for the recovery of the prices alleged to have been agreed on were then threatened by the Company, and a consultation was held by those threatened as to the best way of resisting the demands.

On enquiry, it was found that a large number of other persons had been "had" in a similar way, and at a meeting of those interested which was called, it was resolved to fight the matter out and try and unravel the mystery, it being evident that there was a swindle somewhere. Detective Christie was accordingly requested to try and ferret out the facts and it was not long before he came to the conclusion that the various signatures had been by some means transferred from the list of patrons to the order-form which the canvasser had himself subsequently filled in, inserting in the orders what number of copies he chose. Having arrived at this conclusion, it occurred to the detective that it would be useful, first of all, to endeavour to trace the previous history of the canvasser with a view to ascertaining whether there were in existence any records of his life which would indicate that he would be a person likely to commit such a fraud. After some trouble, it was elicited that this man had before been twice convicted and imprisoned for swindling, and was a very likely person to have committed the forgery.

Having found this out, Christie then called on one of the leading stationers and lithographers of Melbourne, and enquired if there were any known process by which a signature could be transferred from one paper to another, without the fact of its being a transfer merely being apparent. Somewhat to his surprise, he found such was the case, and in response to his request was very kindly instructed in the method by which this result could be obtained. He very soon became expert at the trick, and was able to transfer any signature and reproduce it, so that its genuineness as a signature could not be disputed. Having obtained this information his next step was to have an interview with the canvasser. Christie had a friend who had known this man in his more reputable days, and this friend he asked to meet him, as if by accident, at an hotel where he had found out the canvasser and his associates were in the habit of meeting nightly. It was arranged that the friend should take an opportunity of introducing the detective to the canvasser, Christie being in disguise.

All was arranged accordingly, and in the evening, Christie appeared at the hotel got up with a black curly wig, black moustache waxed and pointed at the ends, eyebrows darkened, and carrying a small Gladstone bag containing an order book and a copy of a book for which he intended to profess to be canvassing; the bag also contained the transferring apparatus. He duly met his friend who, however, so complete was the detective's disguise, did not recognise him till he had disclosed his identity. The two went into the room where the canvasser and his mates were sitting, and Christie then called for champagne, treating his friend as if he were a new acquaintance. Whilst the liquor was being imbibed, he told his friend in tones sufficiently loud to be heard by the others in the room, that he was canvassing for orders for a book, which was then just published, and asked his acquaintance to give him an order for it in his order book, which he also drew from the bag.

The friend then called the canvasser over to their

table and introduced him to Christie, who invited him to sit down with them and join them in a glass of wine. He was then asked by Christie to give an order for the book.

"Oh," he said, "I am in the same line of business myself." Christie's friend then said he would have no objection to sign his name to a list of patrons, but would not undertake to buy any of the books. After signing, the friend, according to previous arrangement, left Christie with the canvasser, who had become much interested and disposed to be "chummy," and enquired of Christie how he managed to be so successful, seeing he could afford to "shout" champagne, especially as he had observed that no order had been got from the man who had just left.

"Well," said the detective, "as you are in the business, I don't mind telling you how I manage it. As you saw, I got that man's signature to a list of patrons; now that was good enough for me, as by that means I can land him with a good order. I have got that in my bag which will do the rest, but how I do it is my secret."

After a little further desultory conversation, Christie remarked that he was waiting for another man he was expecting to meet at the hotel, and as he felt rather tired, he would lie down on the sofa till his expected visitor came. This he did, leaving his bag unlocked on the table. He soon pretended to go to sleep, and then the canvasser and his friends began to converse about him, apparently thinking that he was a little overcome by the wine he had imbibed. On hearing this, the detective began snoring, and the more he snored the less notice they took of him.

At last the canvasser slipped over to the table and, opening the bag, inspected the contents, the sight of the apparatus giving him all the information he desired. When he had got back to his seat, Christie pretended to wake up. On observing that he was awake, the canvasser asked him to come with him into another room where they would be alone.

On arrival there, he closed the door, saying, "I know your little game now. If we go partners and trust each other we can make our fortunes by working together."

"That sounds all right," Christie answered, "but how am I to know that I can trust you with my business and the knowledge of my method of working."

"Well," the other replied, "the fact is, to be quite candid with you, I am on the same 'lay' myself. I have been canvassing for a picture called a 'Cloud of Witnesses,' and unless I am mistaken we are both at the same game."

"Right you are," said Christie, "show me how you do it, and I will show you my method." Smith then produced his bag and explained his process, which was much the same as that which Christie had been taught by the lithographer. They then returned to the other room, where Christie was introduced to the other canvassers, who put him up to various wrinkles and tricks which were practised by them in the course of their business.

The detective then took his leave, after agreeing to meet him at the same hotel on the following evening. He had closely observed his new friend's bag, which he noticed had been placed behind the bar, and next day procured one of the same make and of the same size and appearance in every respect. He then called at the hotel in *propria persona* and asked the landlady, who knew him well, to allow him to leave his bag behind the bar for safety for a short time. To this she civilly assented, and he placed it beside the canvasser's, which was still there.

The landlady shortly afterwards left the bar to get tea, leaving a barmaid in charge, and the girl was then the only other person in the room. Christie then took up ostensibly his own bag but actually the other man's, and carried it into the next room. Nobody being there, he had no difficulty in opening the lock, which was a common one, and emptied all the contents out, returning it empty to its place behind the bar; then, leaving by the back entrance, unknown to the barmaid, he took the contents over to the watch-house and put them into the old bag he had left there. Then returning to the hotel by the same back way, his absence not having been observed in the interval by any one, he remained till the landlady had come back from her tea and then requested her to hand him his bag, and having received it, he sat down awaiting the arrival of the man, who soon turned up, but, of course, did not recognise Christie as the man he had met the previous evening.

Christie was apparently busy but heard him ask the landlady if the gentleman who was in the hotel last evening and had shouted for him had yet come. On her replying in the negative, he said he would do some writing and wait for him. He then took his bag from behind the counter and, placing it on the table, unlocked it. He was evidently dismayed at finding it empty, but thinking he had made a mistake and had taken another bag instead of his own he went to look behind the bar, but, seeing no other there, appeared thunderstruck, saying in agitated tones, "I have been robbed! Someone has opened my bag and stolen what was in it."

The landlady said, "Nonsense, that is impossible; the bag has never been out of the bar or been touched by anyone since you put it there. If, however, you have lost anything, you had better tell the detective sitting over there in the corner," at the same time indicating Christie, who feigned to be entirely unobservant of what was going on. "You had better tell him all about it."

Hearing this, Christie jumped up, and, coming over to the man, asked if he were certain it was his own bag. "Oh, yes," said he, "I know it by the labels on the bottom." Christie then told him enquiries would be made for what he had lost, and then left. Going over to the watch-house, he obtained the bag which contained the missing articles and went home. He then carefully examined what he had brought away, and found the whole swindle exposed. Amongst the papers was the original list of patrons with the authentic signatures, about twenty forged orders, and a complete apparatus for transferring signatures. He then immediately returned to the hotel where he found the canvasser, whom he completely astonished by telling him that all the documents and articles he had lost out of his bag had been recovered. He was evidently struck with admiration at the wonderful promptitude and effectiveness of the Victorian detectives, but his admiration was speedily turned into dismay when the finder proceeded to say:—
"On looking them over, however, I see you have been

practising forgery and that you are a regular swindler. I have, moreover, a statement in writing from a reputable citizen, that you had confided to him the system you practise of forging signatures and your methods in doing it, and that you did so the night before last, at this hotel."

With that the man was overcome with rage, exclaiming excitedly, "I took that damned Yankee for a gentleman and not an informer; however, if he has split on me, the game is up."

"Yes," said Christie, "he has rounded on you properly and more than that he is going to swear an information against you to-morrow morning and take out a warrant for your arrest."

Quite cowed and subdued, he answered, "I will not give any further trouble, but will give myself up at the Court in the morning," and then left the hotel. The detective followed him in a cab to an hotel, where he was apparently staying. He there paid his bill, took his portmanteau and went straight to the Spencer Street Railway Station, and, after waiting some time, took the express train to Sydney.

No further trouble was taken about him, and though the summons had been taken out by the Company against several so-called subscribers yet, in the absence of the prosecutor, they could not be proceeded with. This was, perhaps, fortunate for them, as there would have been considerable difficulty as regards any individual order, in proving that the signature had been transferred, inasmuch as the signature itself was genuine, and many other orders which were really genuine had been given and no direct evidence could be produced in

## "A CLOUD OF WITNESSES."

defence to prove that any individual name had been attached by the process.

As a wind-up to the affair, the Company came to a compromise and agreed to accept a small sum from each of the alleged subscribers in payment of all demands. This settlement was cheerfully agreed to by the victims, who were delighted at escaping so easily.

## CHAPTER XXIV.
### THE "LANGUAGE" OF BIRDS.

AMONGST other duties committed to the Department of Trade and Customs was that of administering the Act of Parliament which provided for the preservation of the native fauna, and Christie was frequently engaged in this work. One day two elderly ladies called at the Customs House and related the following circumstances. They lived in a northern suburb, and said that their neighbours on one side next door were the possessors of a magpie and a cockatoo, and suggested that these birds should be seized, as the possession of such birds was understood to be contrary to the Act. The ladies stated that their reason for asking was that their owners had taught the birds to use the most dreadful language. They said that none of their family could appear without the birds giving utterance to a torrent of bad language. They had applied to the Sergeant of Police, and he had told them he was unable to do anything, as the birds were private property and the place not public.

Christie called at the ladies' house. In order to show what the birds were capable of, one of the ladies, who was red-headed, went into the yard. Immediately, the magpie and cockatoo hopped on their perches and commenced talking.

"Hullo, carrots," said the magpie, "where are you off to? At it again?" When the cockatoo chimed in with, "What the h—— are you going to do?" and so on.

## THE "LANGUAGE" OF BIRDS.

After consultation it was decided to bring the birds to the Customs House. They were placed in the basement, when their language became so loud as to attract a considerable audience of sailors and others who were about the building. The "shell-backs" were experts in language, but owned that the birds were past masters in the art.

It was decided to send the birds to the Curator of the Zoological Gardens. Accordingly a note was written to Mr. Le Sœuf, the curator, informing him that the Department had much pleasure in forwarding for his acceptance two valuable birds, possessed of most extraordinary linguistic attainments. But when the birds were unveiled and restored to daylight, his pleasure soon departed. In a few minutes they had run through their extensive repertory. The horrified curator begged the Inspector to take his infernal birds back again at once, adding that so far from being an attraction they would clear the Gardens of visitors in no time, especially as most of the latter were women and children. There was no alternative but to destroy the talented birds, lest, if they were let loose, they might contaminate all the native birds in Australia.

An amusing incident happened in a Melbourne auction room, showing how "conscience doth make cowards of us all." A talking magpie was offered for sale and knocked down for 12/6 to a purchaser, who wickedly gave his name as Dr. Wollaston. The purchaser, pursuing his little joke at the expense of the auctioneer, inquired, "Is there any risk about this bird?" The auctioner answered, "Well, you ought to know, doctor; but here is Detective Christie coming in at the door, and he can settle the question." The effect was electrical. The apocryphal Dr. Wollaston dropped the cage, protesting that his bid had been mistaken.

On another occasion Christie received a present of a magpie which, in a kerosene tin, was being conveyed by him to his home at Brighton. The tin was placed under one of the seats of the railway carriage, in which were the late Mr. Richard Speight, then Commissioner of Railways, and about half a dozen ladies.

When the train commenced to move hoarse cries were heard to come from behind one of the ladies' petticoats under the seat, and a strident voice yelled out, "What the h——'s that?" The lady gave a scream, and exclaimed, "Oh, there's a man under the seat!" The other women passengers joined in the confusion and hubbub. The bird continued to pour out a string of bad language and remarks uncomplimentary to the fair sex generally, with special reference to their personal appearance. Christie kicked the tin to make the bird "shut up." This, however, seemed only to incite it to more vigorous language. The officer was overwhelmed by the evident disfavour with which he was regarded, and endeavoured to explain that he was in no way responsible for the bird or its language, as he had only just received it as a present.

Before dismissing the subject of talking birds, it may be mentioned that the ex-detective has now in his possession a handsome parrot, which whenever he hears any strong expression of language immediately yells out, "Now then, pull up, pull up."

## CHAPTER XXV.
### CONCLUSION.

THE foregoing pages convey some adequate impression of Detective-Inspector Christie's varied career and experiences. It is surely a unique record for one man in his time to have played on the world's stage such diverse parts as detective, champion boxer and oarsman, Detective-Inspector of Customs, entrepreneur, and Royal "Shadow." His numerous trophies and testimonials are evidence too that he played each part well.

It was undoubtedly a marked distinction for so young a man as Christie to be chosen as "Shadow" to the Duke of Edinburgh, and to have secured the personal esteem of His Royal Highness. He was even more successful in his experience as "Shadow" to Their Majesties the King and Queen when, as Duke and Duchess of York, they visited Australia in 1901 to open the first Parliament of the Commonwealth. He was in attendance upon their Royal Highnesses throughout the Australasian tour on the H.M. royal yatch S.S. *Ophir,* where he was the guest of Commander R. E. Wemyss.

Autographed photographs, medals, and other valuable gifts testify to the regard which his loyalty and diligence inspired. Nor were the authorities who selected him for the special duties of Royal "Shadow" less appreciative of his services, as the following letter shows:—

COMMONWEALTH OF AUSTRALIA.
Department of External Affairs,
Melbourne, 20th August, 1901.

Sir,—

Your services in connection with the visit of Their Royal Highnesses the Duke and Duchess of Cornwall and York to Australasia being now concluded, I am instructed by the Right Honorable The Prime Minister to convey to you the thanks of the Commonwealth Government for the very satisfactory manner in which you discharged the responsible duties which were allotted to you. The practical mark of Their Royal Highnesses' appreciation of your services, too, cannot fail to be a source of much gratification to yourself and to the Service to which you belong.

I have the honor to be, Sir,
Your obedient servant,
(Signed) ATLEE HUNT, Secretary.

J. M. CHRISTIE ESQ.,
Detective-Inspector,
Melbourne.

Mr. Christie's public services on behalf of charities date from the earliest days of his career. He was instrumental in raising over £30,000 in 43 years and entered heart and soul into any movement to succour the distressed or to further a patriotic cause. His work on behalf of the shipwrecked *Dandenong* Fund, the Creswick Mining Disaster, the Patriotic Fund, the Unemployed Fund, and various funds for the help of hospitals and charities generally, has been conspicuous. Four Mayors and Lord Mayors have at different times made him public presentations on behalf of the citizens of Melbourne. The last was upon his retirement from the Commonwealth Public Service, "in recognition," as the Address ran, "of your eminent services as Detective-Inspector of Customs," and "an expression of our keen appreciation of your valuable services in the Department of Trade and Customs of the Commonwealth of Australia and the State of Victoria for such a lengthened period, during which time, in the performance of your important duties, you enjoyed to the fullest extent the confidence and esteem not only of the Government, but also of the general public."

Mr. Christie's retirement was no doubt hastened by the effect of a sensational attack made upon him when in pursuit of opium smugglers. It was a most murderous assault, in which a knife was used. He was rendered unconscious, but fortunately was found in time to receive prompt attention from Surgeon-Colonel Charles Ryan, Surgeon-General Williams, and Dr. Barrett. While he lay ill, daily inquiries were made as to his progress from all quarters, Government House, Parliament House, official circles, and private citizens. He made a complete recovery, and resumed duty, but did not linger in the public service. Upon his retirement, he received the following graceful letter from the Acting Prime Minister of the day:—

COMMONWEALTH OF AUSTRALIA.
Acting Prime Minister,
December, 24/10.

Dear Mr. Christie,—

I feel that after a lifetime spent in the Service of the State your retirement, rendered necessary through injuries received while carrying out the responsible duties of your office, calls for some brief reference from the Government of the day to your many and great services to this country.

And will you let me say too for myself how very much I admire those qualities of courage, tact, tenacity of purpose, unswerving devotion to duty, and unimpeachable integrity which have characterised you throughout the whole of your career.

I hope you may be long spared, and that the effects of the recent cowardly attack upon you may not prove permanent.

The loss to the Department through your retirement will be felt keenly.

Wishing you the happiest of New Years, I am, dear Inspector Christie,

               Yours truly,
               (Signed) W. M. HUGHES.

Similar letters to this might form a book in themselves. Christie has had letters of appreciation even from criminals, whom he has run to earth, thanking him for his gentlemanly manipulation of their personal affairs, which he had brought to a temporary halt. One of these characteristic letters, written on the occasion of a public testimonial to the famous Detective, is reproduced in facsimile in this volume.

An "Old Hand's" Tribute to Detective Christie.

# INDEX.

|   |   |
|---|---|
| Ah Kim | 179 |
| Ah Toon | 175 |
| Albury | 216 |
| *Aldenham, The* | 179 |
| "Alderman" | 40 |
| Alfred, Prince | 73 |
| *Argyle, The* | 106 |
| Arthur | 121, 128, 130 |
| Aspinall, B. C. | 34 |
| Aubrey, Capt. | 91 |
| Baker (*alias* Young) | 31 |
| Bank of Victoria | 42 |
| Barrett, Dr. | 233 |
| Barwon Regatta | 108 |
| Belmore, Countess of | 77 |
| "Ben, the Carpenter" | 29 |
| Bendigo | 50 |
| Beresford, Lord Chas. | 81 |
| Berkshire Pigs | 213 |
| Bitson, Robt. | 47 |
| Bitton, Ned | 92 |
| "Black Albert" | 168 |
| *Blanche,* H.M.S. | 77 |
| "Blueskin" | 164 |
| Boggy Creek Bridge | 131 |
| Bolden's Station | 12 |
| Bowden, Detective | 69 |
| Branch, Bill | 99 |
| Brighton | 102 |
| Brookes, Harry | 27 |
| Brooks, Joseph | 42 |
| Brown, Detective | 30 |
| Buncle, Mr. John | 14 |
| Buninyong | 51 |
| Butler, Mr. Walter | 12 |
| "Cabbage-Tree Ned" | 81 |
| Camperdown | 121 |
| Canterbury | 80 |
| "Captain Scot" | 81 |
| Carlton Gardens | 20 |
| Carter, P. J. | 103, 108 |
| Cassandra | 164 |
| Cazaly, James | 103, 108 |
| Cazaly, John | 103, 105, 108 |
| Challenge Sculls | 108 |
| Chirnside, Mr. | 90 |
| "Cho choo chum" | 21 |
| Creswick Mining Disaster | 232 |
| Christie, Capt. Jas. | 9, 73 |
| "Christie's Hotel" | 9 |
| Cleveland, Miss | 83 |
| Cleveland Bay | 63 |
| "Cloud of Witnesses, The" | 218 |
| Cobden | 121 |
| Cody, Jack | 92 |
| "Coffin" Trick, The | 143 |
| Colac | 121 |
| *Commodore Perry, The* | 11 |
| "Commotion" | 11 |
| "Crimping" | 160 |
| Curran, Tom | 13, 92 |
| Dalmahony, Campbell & Co. | 14 |
| Dalton, Sergeant | 23 |
| Daly, Detective | 49 |
| *Dandenong,* S.S. | 91, 232 |
| Delaney, Tom | 131 |
| "Devil's Punch Bowl, The" | 124 |
| Devine, Ned | 81 |
| Duke and Duchess of York | 84, 231 |
| Duke of Edinburgh | 73 |
| Eastern Market | 19, 55 |
| Edwards (*alias* Brown) | 31 |
| Edwards, Jas. | 103 |
| Edwards, Sid | 104, 108 |
| Emmerson, Mr. J. D. | 163 |
| Ferguson, Lizzie | 42 |
| "Fighting Artilleryman" | 14 |
| *Fiji, The* | 151 |
| Fitzroy Gardens | 74 |
| "Flash Jack" | 164 |
| Free, Mickey | 13 |

## INDEX—Continued.

| | Page | | Page |
|---|---|---|---|
| Galatea, H.M.S. | 73 | Melbourne Club | 74 |
| "Ghost, The" | 164 | Melbourne Regatta | 108 |
| Gibson, Mr. Richd. | 14 | Melville, Miss Emilie | 104 |
| Gippsland Lakes | 12 | Messenger, Charles | 103, 109 |
| Haigh Bros | 35, 55 | Messenger, Jas. Arthur | 103 |
| Halliburton | 24 | "Mickey Free" | 13 |
| Harrington, Detective | 30 | "Moonlighters" | 117 |
| Hartney, Detective | 58 | Moore, Robt. | 84 |
| Hawthorn Bridge | 138 | "Mother" Waddle | 30 |
| Hicken, Abe | 91, 99 | Mount Pleasant | 12 |
| Hopetoun, Earl of | 84, 129 | Murchison | 51 |
| Hudson, Detective | 42 | Murphy | 125 |
| Hughes, Hon. W. M. | 234 | National Bank | 50 |
| Humbug Reach | 105 | New Zealand | 77 |
| Hunt, Mr. Atlee | 232 | Nichol, Capt. | 160 |
| "Jack the Lagger" | 31 | Nicholls, Mr. Arthur | 108 |
| "Jack Sheppard" | 164 | Nicolson, Supt. C. H. | 14 |
| Jones, Constable | 131 | O'Brien | 63 |
| Jones, Dick | 55 | O'Brien, Dennis | 115, 119 |
| Jones, William | 37 | O'Callaghan, Inspector | 134 |
| Kato, Mr. | 50 | O'Grady, Michael | 47 |
| *Keera*, S.S. | 11 | *Ophir*, H.M.S. | 231 |
| Kidney, Driver-Detective | 45 | Opium | 171 |
| Kilmany Park | 11 | Otira Gorge | 81 |
| "Lai Quan" Opium | 175 | Owen, Wm. | 36 |
| Langham, Nat | 10 | Paddy's (Eastern) Market | |
| Lanyon and Bryant | 117 | | 19, 55 |
| "Larrikin" | 23 | Patrick, Capt. | 11 |
| Learmonth | 51 | Patriotic Fund | 232 |
| Lennon, Mr. Hugh | 15 | Pearson, Mr. A. C. | 11 |
| Le Sœuf, Mr. | 229 | Pearson, Mr. Wm. | 11, 13 |
| Lindley, George | 47 | Pigs, Berkshire | 213 |
| *Loch Ard, The* | 115 | "Plausible" | 11 |
| Loch, Low | 218 | Port Melbourne | 168 |
| Long, Ben | 27 | "Port Wine Mary Anne" | 164 |
| Love, Jim | 132 | Princess Theatre | 91 |
| *Lyee-Moon*, S.S. | 109 | Quong Sing | 175 |
| Lyons, Mr. | 158 | *Renown, The* | 165 |
| Lyster, Wm. Saurin | 54 | Reoch, Mr. Hugh | 11 |
| Mace, Jem | 22, 97, 109 | Rodgers | 63 |
| Mainwaring, Detective | 65 | Rogers | 63 |
| Manix, John | 47 | Rose, Alex. | 50 |
| Manners, Sutton, Sir Hy. | 76 | Ryan, Col. Chas. | 233 |
| Maoris | 78 | Sayers, Tom | 10 |
| *Mary Jane, The* | 163 | Secretan, Detective | 57 |
| McEwan | 32 | Seymour | 212 |

## INDEX—Continued.

| | Page | | Page |
|---|---|---|---|
| "Shanghaing" | 160 | Treasury Gardens | 73 |
| Shannon, Jimmy | 167 | Tzar of Russia | 74 |
| Sharp, John | 104 | *Tsinan*, S.S. | 178 |
| Smallpage, Mr. M. | 13 | Unemployed Fund | 232 |
| Smith, Major A. K. | 105 | Walhalla Long Tunnel | 11 |
| Smith, Robt. | 42 | "Wandering Willie" | 11 |
| *Snowbird, The* | 63 | *Warhawk*, S.S. | 106 |
| Snowden, Constable | 131 | Wemyss, Commander R. C. | 231 |
| Spann | 23 | Wellington | 78 |
| Speight, Mr. Richd. | 230 | Western District | 115 |
| Standish, Capt. | 74 | "Whiskey" Creek | 130 |
| Stout, Wm. | 109 | "White-headed Bob" | 47 |
| Stawell, Chief Justice | 13 | Williams, H. A. | 106 |
| Strathfieldsaye | 12 | Williams, Detective | 35 |
| Strike, George | 14 | William, Surg.-Genl. | 233 |
| Stringer's Creek | 12 | Wilson | 126 |
| Summerhayes, Sergeant | 20 | Wilson, Jack | 42 |
| Swears Island | 62 | Wilson, Senr., Jas. | 102 |
| Sydney | 63, 76, 212 | Wilson, John | 97, 109 |
| Theatre Royal | 36 | Wollaston, Dr. (Sir Harry) | |
| Thomas | 31 | | 136, 148, 160 |
| Thompson, Jack | 91, 99, 101 | York, Duke and Duchess of | |
| Thompson, Joe | 91 | | 84, 231 |

237

The "Told-by-the-Pioneers" Series.

Vol. I.

Some Excerpts from
Many Favourable Press Reviews
of

# Recollections of a Victorian Police Officer

by

JOHN SADLEIR,

Ex-Inspecting-Superintendent of Police, Victoria.

320 pages, with over 50 Illustrations. Cloth, 5s. Postage 2d.

"Mr. John Sadleir's qualifications are undoubted. His book therefore may be accepted as authentic history. In addition to these qualifications, he writes in a direct, convincing style, without straining after effect. The events with which he deals are in themselves sufficiently sensational, and, to use a journalistic expression, he 'lets the story tell itself.' He has written in regard to many episodes what no other man could write, and, in producing this book in the evening of life, he has made a very valuable contribution to Victorian history. . . . Mr. Sadleir's is a book one would like to linger over, so full is it of pleasant minor stories that help to make character in our history. There are romantic episodes relating to the early history of country towns, and a great deal of out-of-the-way information respecting administration and social life has been happily rescued from obscurity. The book is copiously illustrated."—*The Argus.*

"As yet Australia has no epic. The material is ready to hand—only the writer is required. The annals of our pioneer days are packed full of stirring incident and romance, and when some genius of the future comes to weave his story around the legendary figures of the past he will surely owe much to such a pioneer as John Sadleir for the quiet, faithful history of what he himself saw and heard during the early days of our colony. . . . Forty years of active service have given him a store of recollections, the publication of which must be of inestimable value to the history of our State. With police organisation, and with criminal outbreaks Mr. Sadleir had, of course, closest connection, but his reminiscences embrace men and matters in every walk of life."—*The Age*.

"Mr. Sadleir's reminiscences are not only vivid and exciting, but present a frank and critical, yet palpably fair, account of the police force which in Victoria's early days bore almost that importance to her existence which a standing army bears to that of older and stronger civilisations. . . . Besides its more graphic passages, the book contains a good deal of valuable criticism on the police organisation of Victoria, past and present, and is written in a simple and manly style which should commend it to every kind of reader."—*Melbourne Herald*.

"A book that will, we doubt not, have a large and appreciative circle of readers now, and will also in time to come take rank among the original sources of early Victorian history. It is written with a straightforward simplicity that carries conviction. No one who reads it can fail to feel its sincerity. The story he has to tell is full of stirring incidents and his narrative gains rather than loses from his restraint of language. Without any attempt at literary embellishment he succeeds in stamping upon a reader's mind picture after picture of bygone scenes and vivid impressions of the men among whom he lived and moved."
—*The Australasian*.

"His was a life full of incident and adventure, a life, moreover, which witnessed tremendous changes in the development of Victoria and brought him into contact with many notabilities now dead and gone. Its story is told in Recollections of a Police Officer, a fascinating book, which gives a graphic picture of the works and days of a member of the force in those far-off times. . . . These interesting pages are the record of a varied and exciting career."—*Sydney Morning Herald*.

"There is certainly not a single dull page in the book, and many are exceedingly interesting as clear-cut, unexaggerated descriptions of incidents such as the sticking-up of the McIvor gold escort by 'Captain' Melville and the hunting and capture of the Kelly Gang. But Mr. Sadleir does not only recount remembered incidents of crime; he made the acquaintance and often won the friendship of public men prominent in law, politics and other pursuits, and these he recalls for us in some graphic pictures, always telling us of their good qualities, yet often not sparing them a record of their defects. Indeed, a noteworthy characteristic of this book is its straightforward, almost daring candour . . . . It is likely that Mr. Sadleir's book will create some stir in political and legal dovecotes. . . . As a record it is of great value and interest, while its descriptions of early days are exceedingly graphic and entertaining. . . . It contains about fifty portraits and other illustrations, which greatly enhance the value of the book and add to its attractiveness."—*Table Talk.*

"There are a number of highly interesting narratives that prove better reading than many modern novels and stories, and as readers may be acquainted with the places, if not the circumstances, there is added interest in their relation."—*Ballarat Courier.*

"The author exhibits an impartiality that makes the authenticity of his writing most acceptable, and should stamp the 'Recollections' as worthy and reliable."—*Benalla Independent.*

"A very interesting book. . . . Valuable as a record, and it should be valuable also to those in the police service through Australia, in that it indicates a good many things which should be avoided. But it must not be thought that Mr. Sadleir 'does a growl' all through. Rather it is otherwise. He hits out very straight at times, but he also gives many illustrations of devotion and splendid courage on the part of the police."—*Brisbane Courier.*

"This interesting volume is one of the 'Told-by-the-Pioneers' series, published by George Robertson and Co., and the excellent get-up of the book, which is well illustrated, reflects great credit on these enterprising publishers. . . . There is much in the book relating to prominent men connected with the police or the law courts, and it will be read with interest by those who care for information about the early days of Victoria."—*Adelaide Mail.*

---

B. R. GOWAN & Co., Printers, 492 Collins St., Melbourne.